ALSO BY MIKE PURDY

Presidential Friendships:
How They Changed History

101 Presidential Insults:
What They Really Thought About Each Other –
and What It Means to Us

Grace in the Wilderness:
The Heart and Mind of Mike Purdy
(Selected Writings)
Volume 1 – Life and Work
Volume 2 – Family
Volume 3 – Theology
Volume 4 – History/Politics & Education

Public Works Resource Guide
Government Construction Contracting

Reflections
of an
Uncertain Journey

MIKE PURDY

Reflections
of an
Uncertain Journey

MIKE PURDY

RANDALL ROAD BOOKS

Seattle • 2023

To my family, friends, and medical providers

who have loved and supported me on this journey.

Holy God of grace and mercy,
we belong to you in body, soul, and spirit.

As we walk this uncertain
and often rocky path,
remind us that you are with us
each step of the way.

Teach us to number our days,
to hold each one lightly,
knowing you are the Lord of the journey.

May we sense and know your calling for us
in this season of life.

Enfold us with your love and
bring us joy on our journey,
even as we experience sadness and grief.

CONTENTS

SPIRITUAL JOURNEY

COMPANIONS FOR THE JOURNEY

MY JOURNEY REMEMBERED

PREFACE

I never wanted to write this book.

Why would I want to write about my failing health with a terminal disease? It's not a comfortable subject. Death isn't a subject any of us want to talk about. We want to press forward, living our lives fully and joyfully, without having to confront the 100% reality that we will all die. Or at least we hope our passage from this world won't be imminent, but at some distant date. We don't want to die at a young age. That's not how things are supposed to be. We're supposed to live a long and productive life.

It's one thing to understand intellectually that we will all die one day. It's quite another, especially for someone in otherwise excellent health, to come to grips with the fact that God's possible timeline for life here on earth could differ from my assumptions and dreams for a long life.

I almost didn't write this book. Most people wouldn't willingly attack a wasp's nest, knowing the result would be countless serious stings. Yet that is what I have done metaphorically with this book. It is painful for me to poke at and stir up the raw emotions of my heart, the fearful thoughts of my mind, the worries and weariness of my spirit, and the unpleasant memories of physical discomfort.

It would have been far easier, in one sense, for me to simply put my head in the sand and not share my journey about the metastatic prostate cancer that has begun to suck the life blood out of my body. Certainly, it would be far easier to simply ignore and suppress my emotions. After all, there are plenty of other subjects about which I would much rather write.

I write this book, however, because, it seems to me, in some small measure, that I might be helped by confronting and framing my mortality in the larger story of human history.

What has really motivated me to write this book, however, is my desire to help others who may be confronting their own life challenges, especially those dealing with the reality that their mortal bodies are failing and their sojourn on this planet may end much sooner than they ever expected. I want my own uncertain journey to help others to live well.

It's easy for me to become self-absorbed and feel sorry for myself about the unfairness of my failing health and worry about how many more days I have here. Occasionally, however, it has occurred to me that perhaps my journey isn't or shouldn't be all about me.

Maybe in God's sovereignty, some of my struggles, reflections, fears, and hopes might inspire others facing similar uncertainties in life.

Left to my own devices, I would not have written this book. If this book can, however, prompt others to face adversity with grace and determination, hope and purpose, I will feel good that somehow my struggles have had a redemptive purpose.

This book also is an important legacy for me to leave behind. I don't want my journey to be forgotten and relegated only to my own memory and the lives of those close to me.

My wise and perceptive counselor warned me that writing this book would be hard, require vulnerability, and rub my emotions raw. She was right. Instead of writing about U.S. presidential history that I enjoy so much and in which I play the role of a teacher, this book placed me in the role of a student.

Despite the challenges, my counselor encouraged me to tell my story. She said it could be a clarifying experience. Reconstructing my treatments and disappointments has been emotionally taxing and painful, and tears have been my constant companion.

None of us knows the number of our days in this life. Having a life-threatening diagnosis makes me feel the intensity of my ever-narrowing number of days. There are so many things I want to still fit into life—things that may or may not happen. I feel like everything is a race against time to accomplish what I want to and feel called to.

I appreciate what former President Ulysses S. Grant faced in his final days in 1885. He had throat cancer, perhaps exacerbated by his cigar-smoking habit. He had been conned and financially ruined by bad investments. Grant poured all his waning energy into writing his memoirs to provide financial stability for his family. It was a race against the clock. Seven days before his journey of life ended, he finished writing what is still regarded today as one of the best memoirs, presidential or otherwise.

My book does not include medical advice. I am not a doctor, and the reader should consult with appropriate medical professionals to discern the best medical treatments. My treatments may not be appropriate in your case. In this book, I share my opinions, my best understanding of various treatments and how I navigated through the confusing world of a life-threatening health diagnosis. I do not address my journey comprehensively, but I have tried to hit the high points. As long as I can, I gladly will try to answer questions from others encountering their own challenging journeys.

I encourage you to read widely and seek medical advice from a variety of traditional and alternative health care providers. It's your life, and while we would like to think someone must have the answers to our condition, everyone has but a piece of the puzzle. It's up to you to figure out your own treatment plan in consultation with the best minds out there.

I have changed the names of some of the medical professionals I discuss in this book. I have done this to protect their privacy and because

I haven't requested their permission to discuss them here. None of them has read this book prior to publication although I will give copies to some of them. Another reason for using pseudonyms is to not embarrass those with whom I have parted company in my treatment. I discuss my reasoning and process for changing health-care providers in later chapters.

The language and theology in this book reflect the fact that my adult life has been grounded in my desire and attempts to live a faith-based life. Even if you don't find yourself in a similar theological space, I hope you can read beyond the references to God and still be helped by my experiences and understanding of this world and the world to come.

References from the Bible are, in most cases, from the Revised Standard Version, a translation I have used since I became a Christian in fall 1972 during my freshman year in college.

This book is the story of my uncertain journey and my uncertain future. I like the word "journey" because it describes so well our existence on this planet from our birth to our death and all the in-between stops. Thus, I have structured the book around different aspects of my journey. Certainly, there is the challenging story about my physical journey as my body has turned on me with rapidly multiplying cells that should be better behaved. Part of my story is about how I have tried to keep my body functioning. The physical journey, however, is more than a physical one. Confronting my mortality is both an emotional roller-coaster and a spiritual mind-bender.

While I have separated the book into different sections, it's hard to not comingle thoughts among these major headings.

You undoubtedly will notice that I discuss certain concepts multiple times in this book. This repetition reflects not only the importance of certain ideas, but also how confusing this new reality is to me.

There is a tension between my faith that grounds me and my doubts, sadness, and fears. I have tried to convey the messy humanity of this uncertain journey in this candid and vulnerable memoir.

How do I live well when the end of my days is approaching? How do I understand what impact I have had and will continue to have on this world? How have the companions I have been blessed with for this journey helped to fortify me throughout my life, but especially in these precious years of vulnerability when I realize I will likely depart from them sooner than I would like? Finally, how do I move forward and live well on this uncertain journey when I don't know how many days I have left?

Please join me on this journey. My hope and prayer is that some of my words might help you live more fully, thankfully, faithfully, and gracefully for however long your journey may last. Onward we go on this grand adventure of life!

Mike Purdy
Seattle, Washington
October 18, 2022

INTRODUCTION

God our Father,
Your power brings us to birth,
Your providence guides our lives,
and by Your command we return to dust.

Catholic Prayer

STORIES

Each of our stories is unique. However, our similarities ground us in our common humanity. We face challenges in life that are the same. We all experience physical pain and discomfort. We all are emotional creatures and experience the turmoil of our souls. We all are spiritual beings and seek to connect with the broader story of our humanity in light of being bound by time and space. Stories are a powerful tool in understanding and approaching life.

This book tells part of my story as I wrestle with the biggest crisis I have ever faced—the surprising and unexpected story of my deteriorating health with a life-threatening illness in the form of prostate cancer that has spread to my bones. It's not a hopeful prognosis.

The words of Frederick Buechner encourage me to tell my story. An author and pastor who passed away in 2022 after 96 years, he once wrote:

> My story is important not because it is mine, God knows, but because if I tell it anything like right, the chances are you will recognize that in many ways it is also yours. Maybe nothing is more

important than that we keep track, you and I, of these stories of who we are and where we have come from and the people we have met along the way because it is precisely through these stories in all their particularity ... that God makes himself known to each of us most powerfully and personally. If this is true, it means that to lose track of our stories is to be profoundly impoverished not only humanly but also spiritually.[1]

Ultimately, I hope my story can provide a framework for others to understand God and begin to glimpse something of his purposes, even in the midst of serious challenges. As I will describe later in this book, however, this unwelcome journey I have been on since mid-2019, has rocked my theological world. It's not been easy.

I have tried to approach my life theologically ever since my freshman year in college when a half-dozen guys in the fraternity I joined invited me to attend a daily Bible study with them. My faith took form and deepened. Later, I even graduated from a theological seminary with the goal of becoming a pastor. Ultimately, I didn't pursue that vocation.

I have been fortunate, therefore, to have good theological grounding. But nothing quite prepared me for the uncharted territory into which I have been thrust with my body not cooperating and pressing me closer to the end of my pilgrimage on this good, but troubled, earth.

QUESTIONS

Especially in this season of my life, I have more questions than I have answers. The questions are ones of purpose and meaning, and I try to figure out answers moment-by-moment. The answers to my questions don't fit into a neat or simplistic box. They're not the size of a tweet. It's hard work to wrestle with deep questions of life, but, in one sense, I feel more alive than I have ever felt. That doesn't mean there aren't tears and sadness. Part of our humanity involves confronting uncomfortable emotions.

Some of the big questions I wrestle with in this season of life are:

- How can I live well in the twilight years of my life, when my world is falling apart, and my days are narrowing ever too quickly?

- How can I live fully and faithfully in the midst of uncertainty and the unexpected?

- How can I live with joy and purpose, despite the sadness that often overwhelms me?

- How can I die well? How do I pass from this world to the next with grace?

- What is God's larger purpose in this uncertain journey of mine?

Throughout this book, I hope to reflect on these questions and maybe even provide some emerging and tentative answers that have slowly helped me crystalize what it means to live well when my world is falling apart.

WORDS

Obituaries for those who die of cancer often include language about the deceased having courageously fought it. The phrase "fighting cancer" troubles me.

Cancer is an aberration from the normal order of cell growth. Without cancerous activity, cells grow and divide and know when to stop replicating. Cancerous cells, however, hijack our bodies. The roaming rogue cells turn against our bodies. They don't know how to stop the uncontrollable growth. They produce more and more cells that eventually crowd out critical organs and other life functions.

While I understand the common descriptions of "fighting cancer," I wonder if such language misses an important point. "Fighting cancer" stirs up images of gladiatorial combat against this insidious disease, as if that alone could allow someone to conquer this cell programming gone wild.

Rather than "fighting cancer," shouldn't we really be thinking more about doing what is helpful to make our bodies healthy and return them to a state of equilibrium? It's not a battle or fight to win. How can we promote peace in all areas of our lives—physical, spiritual, emotional—that will contribute to healing?

Maybe it is more appropriate to state that someone who has passed away from cancer was overtaken by aberrational cells despite their best efforts to promote healing and health. "Fighting cancer" is an easy and memorable phrase that fails to recognize the multifaceted aspects of working to renew our health that can include diet, traditional and alternative treatments, meditation and prayer.

In addition to avoiding language about "fighting cancer," I have tried to banish talking about "my cancer." Such language allows the cancer to have an unnecessary power over me. It's not my cancer. I didn't create it, nor do I welcome it. "My cancer" personalizes the disease rather than recognizing the uncontrolled cell growth is something that is happening to the body I live in.

DYING WELL

A little more than two years after I was diagnosed with roaming rogue cells in my body, I talked with a dear and long-term friend who also has been diagnosed with cancer. I asked her a question my heart had been pondering for some time: What does it mean for me to die well? She observed that we're not really taught how to do this. We go through life avoiding the inevitable end of our pilgrimage on this planet we call Earth. Then she wisely said that if we live well, we will die well.[2]

That thought has stuck with me. It's really about who we are as people and the choices we make in living today that impact how we die, and whether we die well.

As one who has always loved history, I have often said that we make history every day in the small and big choices we make and who we decide to become. The history of our lives is the cumulation of innumerable decisions and actions.

We will pass from this earth in the same way we have lived. It's all about who we are becoming as people. Certainly, the transition from this world is often accompanied by physical pain and suffering. However, while I have breath, I want to live fully and faithfully, trying not to obsess or worry about my impending departure. That is often much easier said than done.

Sometimes, my moments of clear perspective come while I write in my journal, a practice I began in 1975 as a 21-year-old college student. Writing often helps me discover what I think and feel. Sometimes, my journaling comes out in the form of a prayer. In summer 2021, a little more than two years after I was confronted with the bombshell cancer diagnosis, I wrote the following prayer in my journal:

> Oh Lord Jesus, have mercy upon us. You, who with the Father and Spirit, have created our souls to dwell temporarily in these frail and temporal bodies, be present with us in this journey of life, whether it brings joy or sadness, pain or pleasure, hope or disappointment. Enfold us with your everlasting love even as we face stresses and hardship. Help us to live well as though we had another 50 years of life, but also help soften and sensitize our hearts as we prepare for leaving this good earth, whether that's in a year or a decade, that we may also die well, full of faith and hope.[3]

That prayer reflects perhaps one of my saner moments. At other times, my desire to accomplish more consumes me. Perhaps it is my sense of responding to God's call on my life, but then again, maybe it's only my desire to leave an impact on this world.

The author Henri Nouwen wrote:

> The main question is not "How much will we still be able to do during the few years we have left to live?" but rather, "How can we prepare ourselves for our death in such a way that our dying will be a new way for us to send our and God's spirit to those whom we have loved and who have loved us?"[4]

It's a good question. I find that I vacillate between wanting to be productive and preparing for my death. Certainly, this book is a major and important goal of my later years. I want to share my story with others. I know also, though, that I need to focus on preparing to die well and gracefully.

THE GREAT RESET

Shortly after I was diagnosed with cancer, my insightful and deeply spiritual long-time friend, Jo Dee, commented that perhaps the news of my failing health might serve as a reset for my life. Maybe the cancer is just an alarm clock to help me to renew my priorities and listen carefully to what God has called me to in this season. She was right.

I need to focus on what's important in whatever days or months or years I have remaining, and not allow the tyranny of the urgent to consume my days. If God indeed has called me to certain tasks and relationships, and my days are in his hands, I can rest confidently knowing I won't die before the time appointed by him. The cancer has focused and sharpened my perspective and priorities as I realize that the days ahead of me might not be endless and that they may end when I reach my late 60s or early 70s. Maybe I'll live for many years yet to come. My future is uncertain.

I wish I didn't have cancer, but it has helped me to prioritize my life. I have scaled back significantly on consulting work and have focused on writing. I have also spent more time and at a deeper level with others—listening to them and being listened to. Each day, I have asked myself questions about my use of time and whether it holds significance. I have tried to eliminate things that can quickly consume so much of my time.

AN UNFINISHED LIFE

There is a sense in which my life feels unfinished. At a deep and often painful level, I feel I haven't completed or experienced all the things I dream about. I realize the same could be said about any human life regardless of the age at which the earthly sojourn concludes.

A biography of John F. Kennedy by Robert Dallek is titled *An Unfinished Life*. It's a soberingly apt title about a president whose promising life and presidency were cut short by an assassin's bullet, but it also could be the title of any of our lives. Though author J.R.R. Tolkien lived 81 years, some of his writings were unfinished at the time of his passing.

When the day my Creator calls me home to himself and away from this life, will my life be unfinished? Certainly, and I worry about that. I have enough things I want to do to last three lifetimes.

In another sense, however, if the things I still feel called to in this life—loving people and writing—are, in fact, things God has called me to, he will provide me with the days to accomplish them. He is the sovereign of time, history, and all of life. I can rest confidently knowing that he will provide me with the days to complete those tasks and live out those dreams. It is some small comfort though it certainly stretches me to live out my theological understanding of life.

God ordains and numbers our days, and while I know intellectually and theologically that the date of my departure from this life will be at the right time according to my Creator's will, it's still a challenge to live that reality every day when so many aspects of my life seem unfinished still.

In God's economy, there are no unfinished lives, only lives that last for different durations. Maybe it's not the length of my days that matters most but the quality of my years. While I can understand that I still want more time here on earth.

At one point, I was texting with a dear friend about my fear that my life will be cut short before I have finished the work I feel called to. Despite a lifetime of involvement with the church, my friend no longer believes in God or subscribes to organized religion. Certainly, the church has made grievous mistakes over time and has turned off many people. However, my friend continues to be deeply grounded theologically and offered the following encouragement:

> Do you believe, honestly deep down, that you'll be taken before your mission here is complete? Or do you believe you will be given the time to learn and accomplish all you are here to do? If it's the second one, then take comfort. You'll do all you need to before moving on. It's in hands bigger than yours.[5]

My life definitely feels unfinished from my limited perspective. There are always new things on my horizon that I want to do and experience. As long as I have breath and pain has not overtaken me, I will keep pressing onward, sadly aware that at some point, however, my days and dreams will fade and evaporate.

From God's eternal perspective, however, there's a bigger story being written that I don't fully understand.

NUMBERING OUR DAYS

None of this theological understanding changes my daily feelings. I understand my mortality intellectually, but the reality that this body is being ravaged and invaded by cancerous growth prompts my emotions to take over, and my heart fills with deep sadness, caught between a glimmer of God's work in the world and my own fears. I am not ready to leave this life. I see myself as in my prime, confident enough not to wrack myself with feelings of youthful insecurity. I understand my identity and how I fit into the world. I immensely enjoy life and seek joy even on this wild medical adventure. There are still people to love, listen to, counsel, and help. There are more books to read and write. There are places I want to visit and experiences I long to have. I want to feel loved and known by others.

We all live for just a short time on this planet whether our years are few or many. This season of my life feels like a long goodbye. On one hand, I view this advance warning and wakeup call of my mortality as a gift and reminder to me to live fully in the here and now. I have the gift of time to prepare for the end of my days. I can be deliberate and ask what is important. On the other hand, it is emotionally painful to stretch out my physical deterioration and wonder when the day will come that my journey here ends. It's very sad, but I realize it's also part of the normal cycle of life and human history.

My journey has entered the final phase, but I still don't know when I will pass from this life to the next, just as I never knew the number of my days even before I was diagnosed with cancer. I could live another year or maybe 10 more years. It's clear that I have lived more years than I have remaining here on earth. Fortunately, my gracious and loving Creator knows the number of my days. In a mysterious way that I don't fully understand, God has created us for eternity, not for this Earth.

In light of the uncertainty of the length of our lives, how do we live fully and faithfully today? How do we enthusiastically embrace each moment and each encounter with another person as a holy and sacred moment? How do we live as though today might be our last day, and yet plan for living for many more years? It's an uncomfortable tension to live between today and tomorrow and yet be fully present in the moment.

Everything we have in life is entrusted to us on a temporary basis: family, friends, career, money, possessions. It's important that we not hold them too tightly or possessively, but lightly, recognizing that we have them for but a short time. We don't own things, just as we are not owed things. We get so wrapped up in fear of being alone or not having enough money that we sometimes do not appreciate what we do have.

Despite the uncertainties of this scary roller coaster, I feel like I live fully most of the time. My priorities have shifted into a sharper focus. My family has provided love and valuable practical support. Friends have surrounded me and brought meaning, understanding, encouragement, humor, and love to my heart. They have and continue to sustain me on this journey. I have assembled a caring and knowledgeable medical team to help guide me on this journey. My heart is full and overflowing with gratitude.

Like most people, I have had my share of struggles. Sometimes, I think our biggest struggles come when our expectations are dashed. "This isn't how things should be." I didn't ever imagine that my retirement years would be consumed with trying to stay alive and racing against an invisible clock to pack in as much of life as possible before cancerous cells overwhelm and overtake the essential functioning of my body. I never envisioned that my health would tank so suddenly given my otherwise excellent health. It's all been a surprise and a surreal experience.

Regardless of my challenges and unmet expectations, I have been blessed in life in so many ways. My faith has helped ground me. My health has been excellent. I have had multiple and varied successful careers. I have been gifted with family and wonderful friends. I have matured and grown emotionally over the years.

To understand what this uncertain health journey has been like for me, it's important to understand where my journey has taken me thus far. In the next few chapters, I provide autobiographical material to set the context.

MY
JOURNEY PAST

CHAPTER 1

HEALTH HISTORY

There are no guarantees in life.

From my perspective and given the generally accepted risk factors for metastatic prostate cancer, I was an unlikely candidate to develop it. After all, I have been healthy my whole life and have worked hard to take care of myself.

I have always been tall and thin. In high school, I thought it would be cool to play varsity football, so I joined the team at the beginning of my sophomore year. But there were a couple of major problems with my football career.

First, I didn't weigh enough, tipping the scales at 145 pounds which is very light for a six-foot-two plus frame. I tried as hard as I could one summer to eat heartily to gain weight and not get blown off the field. Nothing I did made any difference and I couldn't gain a pound. Having some heft was important for me since I was trying to play the position of tackle.

The other major problem was that I couldn't see well enough without my glasses and wearing them was not safe or advisable. Whether I chose to play tackle or aspired to a tight end or any other position, good eyesight was a necessary requirement.

Thus, being an almost-blind featherweight made football a strange sport for me to attempt. I spent most games warming the bench while heavier and better-sighted guys received accolades for their football feats. I practiced in the heat of the California sun and smog. I banged my head against other helmets. I actually had to replace two helmets as the ones I had cracked. Perhaps more than my helmets cracked! I didn't do myself any favors by pursuing such an ill-fated football career. If I had to do it over again, I wouldn't play football.

However, one of the lasting benefits from my time playing football was the attendant weight training. I worked hard to increase my muscle mass, especially in my arms and chest. At one point, I joined the informal high school 200-pound club—those who could bench-press that amount of weight.

At the end of my junior year of high school, I was elected student body president and quickly used that as my exit strategy from being on the football team my senior year. I was surprised that the head football coach pressured me to not drop football, but I was resolved to put an end to such arduous work without any reward. I told the coach I wanted to focus on being president and wouldn't have time to practice. I feel grateful I had a face-saving means of ending my football career.

My inability to gain weight for football held sway in later years and I have maintained a healthy weight my whole adult life. Also, my blood pressure always has been low, to the envy of others. I have exercised and tried to eat healthy foods. Certainly, sugar has been a weakness of mine. I have never been overweight. I have been limber and have had good strength and endurance. I have never smoked, drunk alcohol, or used drugs. I have always slept well.

In other words, I had none of the high-risk factors for cancer. Yet, somehow, by age 65, I was diagnosed with prostate cancer that had already spread to my tailbone, hips, and pelvic bone.

I have tried to take care of my body over the years as I have been aware that I do not have good family genes. While some of my ancestors died of cancer, a heart attack has concerned me most. I have lived longer than my parents, uncle, and all four grandparents, in addition to most of my great-grandparents and great-great grandparents. Only a few made it into their 70s or 80s, and my great-grandfather, Austin Lynch, lived to be 91 years old, a record in my family's ancestry.

CHAPTER 2

VOCATIONAL HISTORY

All work is holy, sacred, and has intrinsic value
and significance in God's economy.

Mike Purdy[6]

When I was a kid and even through my high-school years, I knew I wanted to be president of the United States. In fact, everyone in my high school assumed that's what I would eventually do, and my yearbook from my senior year includes many notes from classmates expressing their confidence that I would end up in the White House. "I can't wait to see you as U.S. President someday," wrote one classmate. But my vocational journey was different from what I anticipated or what others expected. Life is often like that.

There were other career paths I could have pursued. I could have become an attorney, except in those critical college years, I was somewhat clueless about how to go to law school or what a legal career would entail. I also could have become a pastor. Or with more career guidance in my high-school and college years, I might have become a history professor, reflecting a lifelong passion and interest in U.S. history.

Instead, my career choices were driven by pragmatism instead of passion. I chose to major in business and public administration, a practical degree. I didn't really know to which jobs such a degree might lead me, but it seemed like the right decision at the time. In retrospect, I see that God was at work in using that to help shape me and my career.

My degree in business and public administration focused on marketing, but I knew I didn't want to spend a career working for a company increasing the consumption of potato chips or pickles. Instead, I decided to pursue a career in public service, first as a university administrator and then as a government employee.

After I graduated from college in 1976 with my undergraduate degree, Mom wanted me to move back to Southern California, and so I did. I spent that summer floundering, confused, and depressed. I had job offers ranging from selling insurance to being a retail worker for a large department store. None of those was appealing to me. I almost became a graphic-design artist, making it to a second interview with the University of Southern California during which I provided a mockup of a newsletter. I didn't get the job. Applying for jobs required money for gas in those pre-internet days where nothing was done online, so I became a short-order cook at a Mexican fast-food restaurant on Colorado Boulevard in Pasadena. The owner was impressed with my skills and offered me a job managing one of his other stores. I turned it down. I hadn't gone to college to pursue that kind of career.

Finally, in late August 1976, after reaching out to my alma mater, the University of Puget Sound, I was offered a job helping to manage the admissions and registration process at the university's branch campus in downtown Seattle. I quickly packed my not always reliable 1956 Chevy and drove back to Tacoma on a trip that included some harrowing fog through Oregon's Siskiyou mountains.

I had no experience with the subject matter, but to the university administrators, I was a known quantity. Eventually, I became assistant director for the university's Olympia campus, which I was primarily responsible for managing.

I soon realized, however, that I would never be able to advance, either at the university or with another employer without a graduate degree. I enrolled in the university's MBA program and completed the degree in nine months.

After obtaining my MBA in 1979, I applied for other jobs, mainly in the public sector. Eventually, I was hired by the City of Seattle Board of Public Works as second-in-command of a small department. My supervisor was insecure and not a good communicator.

After almost a year, I was looking for an exit strategy when my boss called me into her office. I was scared. This was the equivalent of being summoned to the principal's office in school—never a good sign. Instead, she informed me she was retiring. I was ecstatic.

After she retired, I was appointed as acting head of the department. It meant, among other things, attending the cabinet meetings of the mayor as a 26-year-old, along with other city department heads, all of whom were older, and much more experienced and confident than I was.

After two years in an acting capacity, I was passed over for the permanent position for a more experienced manager. The disappointment was tempered by the birth of my first child within days of the news I would be going back to my former position. For the next 11 years, I was privileged to work with my new boss, Barbara Taber, who taught me so much about what a good manager should be. We enjoyed a wonderful partnership, and she provided me with much-needed schedule flexibility to pursue my Master of Divinity degree while still working.

My job with the City of Seattle lasted 21 years through various reorganizations and promotions, and I developed expertise in contracting issues for public construction projects. From there, I joined the Seattle Housing Authority as procurement and contracting manager. After five years there, I left for a similar position at the University of Washington's

Capital Projects Office. That position expanded my statewide profile and involvement with legislative issues.

While I was at the Seattle Housing Authority, I began private consulting work for public agencies in the area of construction and consultant contracting. While I was at the University of Washington, my consulting workload began to expand, and I found I was using up all my available vacation time to pursue consultant opportunities.

When I retired after 30 years working for government agencies in 2010, the floodgates of consultant work widened. I spent the next decade traveling around the United States and Canada training and consulting for more than 100 public agencies, contractors, architects, engineers, and non-profit organizations. I retired shortly before my 56th birthday, hopeful the early departure from stressful work would be beneficial to my health. Perhaps it was, but not enough, given the cancer diagnosis. When COVID-19 hit in March 2020 and with my focus on maintaining my health after the cancer diagnosis, I began to scale back on consulting.

In 2014, while consulting, I decided to plunge into a lifelong passion of mine related to U.S. presidential history. I hung up my shingle as a presidential historian with a website called PresidentialHistory.com, launching yet another career. It has been one of the most pleasant and amazing surprises of my life that I could, without any academic credentials in history, become recognized in a small way as a presidential historian.

In 2016, I delivered a series of well-received lectures at the University of Puget Sound with a good friend, political-science professor Dr. Michael Artime, about the 2016 presidential campaign. Because the campaign was so unprecedented, I found the news media were very interested in interviewing experts and I have been interviewed by more than 50 national and international media outlets, including CNN, *The New York Times, The Wall Street Journal, USA Today, Newsweek, Reader's Digest,* Associated Press, and BBC.

Whenever I speak in a radio or television interview, I feel nervous, especially for television, for which I must stare at the small-dot camera on my laptop, look engaged and somehow find intelligent things to say without stumbling over my words, all without the ability to look at my notes. At least with a radio interview, I can look at notes I have prepared. But the interviewer still might ask me questions about which I have not prepared.

I have had articles published online at The Hill, History News Network, and *American Heritage* magazine. It has been gratifying to have friends encourage me to continue to write and be a voice of reason in our polarized political world. As long as I have breath, I will continue to do so. It seems to be part of my calling and I want to have a positive impact on our world.

I have written and published two books about the presidents that I discuss more in Chapter 33.

My career as a presidential historian has been the most fun of any of my vocations. It has been pure joy for me to research, write, and speak about the presidents. It also has been the least financially lucrative of my careers, but that's okay. I have been pleasantly surprised by how I have been able to take my lifelong interest in the presidents and turn it into a national platform.

CHAPTER 3

FAITH HISTORY

Faith, in the sense in which I am here using the word, is the art of holding on to things your reason has once accepted, in spite of your changing moods.[7]

C.S. Lewis
Mere Christianity

Neither of my parents was religious. Whatever faith they had was not the driving influence of their lives.

My paternal grandfather was born into a Jewish family that had emigrated from Russia. About my paternal grandmother, I know only that her ancestors came from Hungary to the United States. My dad, like his parents, lived a secular lifestyle.

My mom's family also had Jewish roots. Her maternal grandparents were active in the Jewish temple in Canton, Ohio. Her paternal grandparents were devout Catholics, so when my grandmother Evalyn and grandfather Edward married, they decided to give up their respective Jewish and Catholic backgrounds. Thus, Mom was raised in a non-religious home.

When I was eight or nine and living in Princeton, New Jersey, Mom took me to a Unitarian church. It was the first time I attended a religious service. I remember Mom saying that the Unitarian church didn't tell you what you had to believe, and that you were free to form your own opinions. I was appalled that some people would attempt to coerce their beliefs on others. It offended my sense of what was right. It was, I think, the beginning of my lifelong passion to think for myself. I resolved that no one ever would tell me what to think and that I would make my own decisions.

Mom gave me a penny to put into the offering plate as it was passed along the pews. I attended only once with her. Whether she went on her own at other times, I don't remember, but this brief experience has stuck with me through the decades.

Another time I was inside a church building also came in Princeton. Mom enrolled me in piano lessons, taught by Mr. Rudy, the organist at Trinity Church, an Episcopal congregation in the historic downtown core, where my lessons were held. However, neither the music nor the environment of faith rubbed off on me. I was a reluctant student and resisted practicing. Reading musical notes was hard for my young brain. Mom soon realized it was an uphill battle to turn me into a pianist, and she gave way to the inevitable and stopped my piano lessons.

I was oblivious to the fact the short-lived lessons were held in a stately 1870 stone Gothic-style building where generations of faithful Christians had worshipped. Just as music failed to penetrate my brain then, neither did the grandeur of the surroundings make any impression on me theologically.

It was also in Princeton where I got into trouble in my third-grade public-school classroom for not being properly reverential during class prayer time. I understood enough about the U.S. Constitution to know that I was guaranteed freedom of religion. So, when my teacher, Mrs. Weiland, invited my fellow students and me to close our eyes to pray, I kept mine open. No one was going to force me to believe anything I didn't want to believe. Apparently, another student, who had apparently deputized himself as the prayer police, also had his eyes open and he noticed my lack of a prayerful posture. He reported me to the teacher who talked with my parents about it. I don't know exactly what transpired next, but I didn't have to conform. Even then, I was fiercely independent about matters of faith.

By my teenage years, I was beginning to think tentatively about matters of faith. Shortly before I turned 14, Mom and my stepfather, Stew, began attending an Episcopal church in San Gabriel, California, near where we lived in San Marino. I regularly attended with them at the Church of the Saviour. It was a new experience for me.

I wrote in a self-portrait paper for my eighth grade English class that "I am a very religious person, more so than anyone else my age," although I don't remember what I was thinking. I also noted that "religion had not meant much to me before" I began to attend the worship services. But my understanding of God and matters of faith were quite elementary and unsophisticated.

My most vivid memory of attending those Episcopal worship services with Mom and Stew was that I regularly got hot, dizzy, and faint from kneeling and standing, making it an uncomfortable experience and one that I came to dread each week. But somehow, I trust that God was at work, beginning to expose my heart and mind to the message of the Christian faith.

When I was 15, I requested a Bible for Christmas. Mom wrapped a black-covered King James Version Bible with a zipper and placed it under the Christmas tree for me. I don't remember what prompted me to make such a request. I don't think I read it much.

During my senior year in high school, I frequently attended weekly Young Life meetings held at homes of other students. They were well attended, and I probably went more for the interactions with my fellow classmates than for the faith-based teaching. Nevertheless, my exposure to the messages began to shape my heart in ways I didn't fully understand at the time.

When I went away to college, I chose to attend the University of Puget Sound in Tacoma, Washington, a place I hadn't visited prior to applying or before my freshman year began in fall 1972. I never had been the partying type, but I went through the Greek rush process to join a fraternity. As I visited the last house, I had resolved that if it wasn't any more appealing than the other houses I had visited, I would not join one. But this one seemed different. In some ways it was, and in other ways, it was typical of all fraternities. I joined Phi Delta Theta.

Shortly into that first term, I was asked by another member of the fraternity if I was a Christian. I didn't really know how to answer his question. I stumbled out an awkward "Yes, I think I am." Everyone in the country was a Christian, weren't they? Or so I thought. Peter invited me to join him and about a half-dozen other guys who met every weekday morning for 30 minutes in one of their rooms for a Bible study and prayer time. I accepted the invitation. It was a new experience for me to be regularly and thoughtfully exposed to the Bible.

Over the course of a month, I began to understand some of the message of the Christian faith. I realized my life was being transformed as my theology and understanding of scripture were being expanded and internalized in my heart and mind. It was a formative experience. The friendship and fellowship of these committed Christians who took me under their wing helped me to grow in my faith in ways I never had before.

During Thanksgiving vacation in 1972, when I was back home in Southern California, I went to Vroman's Bookstore in Pasadena and purchased a black leather Revised Standard Version Bible and had my name imprinted on the cover. That is still the Bible I use a half-century later.

It was during my college years that my faith took root. Outside of the fraternity, I met other committed Christians, many of whom became lifelong friends. I attended weekly large-group meetings for singing, praying, and teaching. Soon I was thrust into a leadership position with the campus fellowship group. I began studying the Bible on my own and helped to nurture the faith of others.

A key event for me occurred when InterVarsity Christian Fellowship, a national organization on college campuses, sent staff workers to the University of Puget Sound. I learned from them and from conferences I attended during breaks and in the summer. InterVarsity helped me appreciate that my newfound faith had intellectual integrity, was founded on historical facts, and did not constitute a blind leap. My faith was taking root and beginning to shape my decisions. I now owned my faith in ways that I never had before.

After I graduated from college in 1976, I became involved in various local congregations in which I frequently taught adult Christian education classes. Was God calling me to pursue a pastoral ministry? I wasn't sure. In fall 1983, I decided to begin taking classes at the Seattle extension program of Fuller Theological Seminary as part of pursuing a Master of Divinity degree that would enable me to become a church pastor. While I worked full-time for the City of Seattle as a contracting manager, I attended classes at night.

After seven years of part-time studying, I completed my degree. By then, however, it was clear to me that God was not calling me to a pastoral ministry in a church. Rather, I came to realize that my work as a manager was pastoral work. Obtaining formal theological education further grounded my faith, something for which I am grateful.

Living faithfully in this world as one who follows Jesus has been my driving passion as an adult. I have come to live by the adage that ultimately all of life is theological. It's not always been an easy journey. But I feel thankful for the ways in which my faith has been nurtured over the years. As I will discuss later, this book is my attempt to grapple with cancer from a theological perspective. There are no easy answers.

CHAPTER 4

EMOTIONAL HISTORY

The only journey is the one within.

Rainer Maria Rilke

Somewhere over the years, I have grown from a shy kid and an insecure young adult into a confident mature man. It's been a surprising journey for me. I still try to figure out where I fall on the introversion-extroversion scale. Friends call me an extrovert and there is truth to that, but I also can enjoy and be energized by time alone. Few of us are pure introverts or extroverts. We're all somewhere along the spectrum.

When I began what was then called nursery school as a young boy (what today we would call preschool), I was painfully shy. On my first day of school, after my mother deposited me there, I was petrified. I wasn't used to interacting with so many other kids. I was insecure. My response to this new environment was to hide in the school's coat closet. I refused to come out of my safe space the whole day. Mercifully, I don't remember the intensity of my fears, but obviously it was a traumatic experience, one that I remember a lifetime later. I presume the remaining days of this school experience went more smoothly. I wasn't naturally an extrovert. I was withdrawn, self-conscious, and cautious.

In my early teenage years, my brother, Steve, and I were playing a game of hide and seek. I sought refuge in the outside entry basement to the duplex Mom had rented in West Los Angeles. I went down the steep concrete steps and once at the bottom, I stepped aside around the corner with my back up against the wall, hiding silently in the dark. Steve came looking for me and had in his hands a BB rifle. As he got to the bottom of the darkened stairs, he swung the rifle around the corner to make sure I wasn't there. I was. It was a direct and powerful hit on my upper front tooth that chipped from the force of the blow. I was in pain, but more than that, I was emotionally devastated by this permanent injury and cried buckets of tears.

For the next dozen years or so, I lived with the chipped tooth since Mom didn't have the money to get it fixed. I was self-conscious. It impacted how much I smiled. Somehow, I overcame this injury and became active and involved in a variety of school and community activities, but the chipped tooth had a deep, personal impact on me.

For many years as a young adult, loneliness defined my life. I found myself distant from others, unappreciated, and lacking confidence.

As I have had successes in school and then in my career, I began to grow in confidence while still introverted. It was only in my 50s and 60s that I began to realize that I was not a pure introvert but had major strains of extroversion built into my psyche. I found I enjoyed people and thrived on interactions with others. I enjoyed meeting new people and engaging them in conversations, listening to them, and asking questions.

PHYSICAL JOURNEY

CHAPTER 5

DIAGNOSIS

Lord, in the midst of the violent storms of life, give me strength, peace, courage, and grace to live as one who belongs to you in body, soul, and spirit.

Mike Purdy[8]

On April 10, 2019, I reached the milestone Medicare age of 65 in seemingly excellent health. I had made it more or less intact, or so I thought.

However, a few months before my birthday I began to experience a surprising onslaught of pains and discomforts that came and went or just stayed. I felt cramps and pressure in my pelvis, groin, and bladder. I was constipated and bloated. The urge to urinate came on often and suddenly and at times was accompanied by sharp pain. Sometimes I felt pressure to urinate but couldn't get anything out. My right hip hurt, and it impacted my daily exercise of walking at times. I had shooting pains in my upper right leg. My tailbone hurt. I experienced a dull scrotum pain. These were all new to me.

Initially, I dismissed these pains as but minor and temporary signs of being in my mid-60s. But they persisted and I reluctantly admitted that perhaps something more serious was going on and I should have my symptoms evaluated by my doctor.

At the time, my wife, Catherine, and I were living in Alaska where she was the daily childcare provider for our then-two-year-old grandson. I regularly flew between Juneau and Seattle for meetings with clients for my consulting business, and to keep tabs on our house. I made an appointment for late March with Dr. Carter, my primary-care physician in Seattle, for a day when I would be in town for other non-medical appointments. I had seen Dr. Carter previously for minor issues and had a high degree of confidence in his expertise as well as his communication style.

At my March 27 appointment, Dr. Carter noted my prostate was enlarged and irregular, something that often occurs as men age. He ran some blood tests. The following day, the results were in. My PSA (prostate specific antigen), which essentially measures the presence of prostate-cancer activity in the bloodstream, was significantly elevated. Any reading of 4.5 or less is considered normal.[9] Mine came in at a shockingly high 65.2. This was scary news.

Dr. Carter and I talked on the phone. He suggested we wait a month and run the PSA test again since inflammation in the body can sometimes result in a high PSA, just as a digital rectal exam, which the doctor performed prior to the blood test, also can elevate the PSA. But he also noted that it was quite possible the elevated PSA reflected prostate cancer.

In early April 2019, I flew to Philadelphia where I attended the annual conference of the Organization of American Historians. I was in significant pain standing and walking around the conference. My legs and hips hurt, which I learned later was likely the result of pinched nerves from the growing cancer. The pain impacted my ability to enjoy the event. I cut short some of my interactions with other attendees. I was too uncomfortable to stand and walk. Something clearly wasn't right with my body.

My primary-care physician referred me to two specialists—a general surgeon to assess whether a hernia was a possible explanation for my symptoms (I didn't have a hernia), and a urologist to discuss possible prostate cancer. I made the appointments for the last day of April. In addition to these appointments on April 30, 2019, I also had a follow-up PSA test. The result was not encouraging. It showed that my PSA had increased from 65.2 at the end of March to 77.2. This most likely reflected that the cause was prostate cancer as opposed to inflammation.

On May 8, just short of a month after my birthday and a few days after a short trip to Boise, Idaho, where I taught an all-day class on government construction contracting, I reported to a hospital in Seattle for a CT scan of my pelvis and abdomen, along with a bone scan. These were new and scary procedures to me, especially since my otherwise excellent health meant that I had spent very little time in hospitals or with medical professionals.

The urologist, Dr. Zarker, called me immediately after reading the scan results that day to speak the dreaded words that no one ever wants to hear: "You have prostate cancer, and it has spread outside the prostate." I was stunned and deeply saddened by what seemed like a death sentence. How did this happen? How could I suddenly go from the picture of health to stage 4 cancer in such a short span with cancer having metastasized to my tailbone, hips, and pelvic bones?

It had been just two months or so since my body started telling me something was wrong before I met with Dr. Carter. Should I have acted more quickly? Maybe, but I was busy with consulting and with marketing a book I had just written about insults our presidents have lobbed at one another and the need for civility in our public and private discourse.[10] My life was full, and it felt like an appointment with a doctor would be a distraction.

Would it have made any difference had I gone in immediately after I started noticing the pains? Probably not. The symptoms reflected a cancer that had been growing for some time. What might have made a difference in my long-term health is if my doctors had regularly ordered PSA tests over the years.

Prior to the PSA tests in 2019 and just before I was diagnosed with prostate cancer, the last time I had a PSA test was in 2006 when it was a healthy 2.6. After 2006, my health-care providers apparently didn't view PSA testing as a recommended or necessary practice. I was relatively young and healthy, and prostate cancer was a foreign concept to me. Unfortunately, I wasn't educated or knowledgeable enough to insist on regular PSA tests. Regular PSA tests could have identified the cancer before it escaped from the prostate and took up lethal residence in my bones.

Some medical providers have felt that PSA testing was controversial because there could be false readings, and a high PSA would force men into deciding whether to take further steps such as a biopsy with risks of infection. The lack of PSA testing was further complicated in 2012 when the U.S. Preventive Services Task Force (USPSTF) recommended against routine PSA screening. It wasn't until 2018 that the USPSTF updated its guidance to suggest that PSA testing for men between ages 55 and 69 should be an individual decision.[11]

So, from my 2006 PSA test until my diagnosis in 2019, the medical world didn't view PSA tests as something that should be done annually. Whenever I talk with men now, I strongly encourage them to insist on an annual PSA test. It is a simple, inexpensive, pain-free, and low-risk blood test. Certainly, there can be false positives, but no one is forced into a biopsy or treatment without evaluating the information. To not systematically collect information about your PSA levels is akin to putting your head in the sand. More information is better.

If I had regular PSA tests starting in 2007, it is likely such tests would have caught the growing cancer before it had metastasized to my bones. There are far more treatments available and a higher rate of success and longevity if prostate cancer is caught early and not allowed to spread.

Many men will be diagnosed with prostate cancer each year. Fortunately for most of them, the cancer grows slowly and remains contained within the prostate. They eventually will die of something else. The

rogue cells found in my body were aggressive and h
prostate, making my long-term prognosis range fron
right depressing. Once cancer has escaped from the ¡
or organs, the world of oncology has no tools to cure
it can do is try to suppress the cancer and keep patien
long as possible.

Since that May 8 conversation with the urologist when he informed me that my body was out of kilter and cancer was on the move inside me, I have been tightly strapped onto a never-ending roller coaster. My wild ride has brought nothing but uncertainty as my body, spirit, and emotions have been jerked around. Coming to terms with this new reality has been a surreal experience for me. How could this be happening to me? It continues to reorder my world daily as I realize that a fuzzy and difficult-to-read expiration date has been stamped on my body.

I continue to be mystified as to the cause of the cancer given my otherwise excellent health. Men with a higher risk of developing prostate cancer include those with a family history of the disease (or other cancers), men of African descent, men who smoke, and men who are overweight.[12] My mother probably had lung cancer, and my father had a blood cancer (chronic lymphocytic leukemia), but there are a lot more heart attacks and strokes in my family history. A couple of distant cousins died of prostate cancer. Thus, I don't have any risk factors typically associated with prostate cancer, let alone cancer that has metastasized.

My future—like for all of us really—is uncertain, since, at some point the medical world will run out of treatments or the treatments will stop working and the cancer will continue its relentless invasion of my bones and eventually my organs. We're all born into this world immediately moving toward the inevitable end of our earthly existence. These bodies are pre-programmed to fail, and that happens at different ages and with varying breakdowns, eventually leading us onto a new grand adventure of a different existence about which none of us knows the details. The cancer jacked the body God has entrusted to me to inhabit on this earthly journey has highlighted for me the transience of human life like nothing else has ever done.

Whatever ailments you may be experiencing, I encourage you to listen carefully to your body. You know it better than anyone else. You know what is normal and what isn't. Don't hesitate to seek medical advice if you are experiencing unusual symptoms. Sometimes, things may be easily resolved. But as these durable yet fragile bodies age, things begin to short-circuit, and it's important to address these concerns in a timely manner.

One moment my life seemed endless. The next moment I was thrust into wondering how many more days I had. All I know in this season of uncertainty, and while my life lasts, is that I want to make a positive difference in the world.

As I began to adapt to a new reality in my life, I resolved to do whatever I could to give my body the best chance to deal with the cancer. I have tried to blend both traditional (often referred to as Western medicine) treatments with complimentary or alternative treatments.

CHAPTER 6

TRADITIONAL TREATMENTS

All therapies work on some patients but not on others.
Medicine offers no guarantees.

Ken Follett[13]

MEDICAL TEAM

Little did I realize when I was diagnosed with metastatic prostate cancer that it would be important for me to assemble a team of medical professionals from various disciplines to help guide me on this health journey. Since I have been healthy my whole life, I haven't had a lot of experience with doctors and the various specialties. In addition, once I made the decision to pursue alternative treatments as well as traditional Western medicine, the number of medical professionals who would be part of my team soared.

While dealing with my health issues, I found some health-care professionals were no longer meeting my needs. Thus, I parted company with a counselor, urologist, oncologist, naturopathic doctor, and nutritional healer.

In addition to the team of traditional and alternative medicine, God has been my constant companion, and I feel grateful for his presence in my life and in shaping my heart as I face this life-threatening illness. He is the great healer.

Scripture, especially the Psalms, have taken on new meaning for me. "O my God, take me not hence in the midst of my days, thou whose years endure throughout all generations." (Psalm 102:24). I have been journaling more consistently—a practice I started in 1975, although there have been times during those years when I haven't journaled daily given other busy aspects of life. I find that journaling helps me to name my fears and figure out my feelings.

EVALUATING TREATMENT OPTIONS

Along the way, I have learned that doctors use three main tests to assess my condition and evaluate treatment options.

First, they look at whether my PSA is going up or down. My PSA has fluctuated over time, but unfortunately, the general trend line has been up, and that has led to different treatment options over time.

Second, they evaluate the results of periodic CT and bone scans to assess whether the cancer lesions are growing, shrinking, or remaining stable. I have had many such scans as they reflect what the growth of the cancer looks like inside my body. The doctor compares the most recent scans with previous ones to assess the status of the cancerous activity. Like the PSA, and consistent with the nature of metastatic prostate cancer, the size and location of the cancerous lesions has grown over time. By mid-August 2022, scans showed the cancer had spread to new areas—not a promising sign.

Finally, the doctors want to know how I feel. Sometimes, I have been feeling good even though the PSA and scans have not been promising. At other times, the discomfort and pain from the growth of the cancer have been a challenge.

The combination of this three-prong approach helps inform my doctors what should be done next.

STARVING THE CANCER

On May 9, 2019, the day after the dreaded diagnosis, I received my first treatment (an injection) designed to help control the cancer cells by depriving them of their primary food—testosterone. The first line of defense in treating metastatic prostate cancer is a set of tools known as Androgen Depravation Therapy (ADT). It is also known as hormone therapy. The idea is to block the production of testosterone to starve the cancer, decrease it, and keep it at bay for as long as possible before the body figures out a way to work around it and create its own testosterone to feed the cancer. ADT comes in injections and oral medications.

The injection of a medication called Lupron which I first had that day in May, takes just a minute. Other than the initial mild pain of a needle being poked into my upper buttocks and sometimes soreness in the days following, it is usually not an uncomfortable experience. I have been blessed to have an experienced and caring nurse, Esma, who has administered most of these monthly treatments.

One side effect of Lupron is hot flashes, and I have experienced them. They've been mildly annoying, but manageable. Another side effect is fatigue. Sometimes it's been hard for me to discern whether my fatigue is due to the Lupron, other hormone therapy, or chemotherapy.

I still go in every month for the Lupron injection to keep my testosterone low. I was encouraged by what my urologist told me about Lupron. He said it has a 95% success rate in lowering PSA levels by suppressing production of testosterone. Over time, the Lupron has worked to keep my testosterone so low that they can't put a number on it.

Within two months of the first Lupron injection, my PSA had plummeted from 77.2 at the end of April to a respectable and normal 3.58 on

July 10, 2019. I was astounded, ecstatic, and grateful at this promising turn of events. This (to be in the normal range and not in the 40s, which is where the doctor said it would be) was the best result for which I could have hoped and prayed. But, while I was thrilled, I also was aware that I was far from out of the woods.

On September 10, my PSA had dropped even further, to 2.92. The Lupron injections were clearly effective in keeping the cancer at bay.

With this amazing success at controlling the PSA, and therefore the cancer, my urologist directed that I should take a one month break from Lupron injections. In retrospect, that seems to have been a mistake. Even now, my oncologist has recommended I continue with the Lupron injections every month to not allow the testosterone to flourish and feed the rogue cells. At the time, I was green about navigating medical issues, so I accepted Dr. Zarker's direction without question.

At the end of the one-month trial of not getting a Lupron injection, my PSA skyrocketed from 2.92 to 17.9. A day later, I resumed the injection but a week after the resumption of the injection, the PSA had gone up yet again, to 29.6. My PSA has never gone down again to the 2.92 from early September 2019 but did slowly stabilize below 4.5 until April 2020 when it began rising outside the normal range.

The one-month gap in Lupron injections and the subsequent rise of my PSA were causing me to grow skeptical of my urologist's treatment plan. I emailed him to ask him what stage cancer I had and what the survival rates were. Surprisingly, in the half year of being treated by him, he had never shared this information. The email response back was blunt and void of any emotion. I had stage 4 cancer. He wrote that "roughly 70% of patients will die within 5 years of the diagnosis of distant metastatic prostate cancer." He provided a link to the American Cancer Society website to support this information.

I immediately requested a referral to an oncologist. Interestingly, when I first began meeting with the urologist, he told me that he could refer me to an oncologist but that all they would do was pump me full of chemo. The way he characterized my choice made it clear to me at that point that seeing an oncologist wasn't something I should do. It seems to me now that he should have been more objective in describing my choice. Given the metastatic nature of the cancer, the urologist should have strongly recommended I be treated by an oncologist since they have more tools available to them than a urologist does for treating cancer.

Since I was healthy for most of my life, I didn't have much experience with doctors. I thought I could rely on everything they said. It was beginning to dawn on me that I would need to be more involved in my treatment and couldn't automatically rely on what I was being told without questioning it.

On October 14, 2019, some five months after I was diagnosed with metastatic prostate cancer, I met with an oncologist, Dr. Austin, for the first time. Initially, I was quite pleased with the guidance and calm manner of this young doctor. It soon became apparent, however, that he always gave short and perfunctory answers to my questions. I got to the point where I could accurately predict his vague and evasive responses. It was hard to get specific information from him other than answers that everything was variable. While I can appreciate the variability of treatments and patient responses to treatments, soon I was frustrated not to be able to get useful information from him.

At that first meeting with Dr. Austin, when I brought up the dismal survival rates that the urologist had referenced, he said that those were outdated, and the prognosis was much better. He said that only 20% of men diagnosed with metastatic prostate cancer would be dead in five years instead of the 70% the urologist had noted. The doctor did not share the source of his more promising statistics.

When I researched survival rates online in spring 2022, everything still pointed to 70% of men being dead in five years. It has now been more than three and a half years since my diagnosis. I realize no one is just a statistic, and that an indeterminate percentage of men with metastatic prostate cancer will survive more than five years, but I also know the clock is ticking on my life, as it is for all of us.

I brought up the survival rates with my then new oncologist, Dr. Percy, in May 2022. She confirmed the 70% mortality rate in five years was based on outdated U.S. information. The more promising 20% mortality rate is based on United Kingdom data that derive from a centralized database that is updated more frequently. This was encouraging.

Regardless of the survival rates, I know that a lot of variables go into those percentages. The statistics encompass men of varying ages and overall health, and don't seem to measure the impact of nutrition, exercise, weight, and supplements. Nevertheless, the survival rates are sobering, and impress on me more and more the preciousness and fragility of human life.

In spring 2020, I shared with my naturopath, Dr. Buckle, that I vacillated between hope and despair about my health. She shared with me that she was cautiously optimistic about me on the bell curve of longevity, because I do things to promote my health that very few other men with prostate cancer do. Dr. Buckle's perspective is encouraging, a good thing for me to remember when I get caught up in worrying. I continually remind myself of the words of the psalmist that "my times are in thy hands." (Psalm 31:15).

My oncologist, Dr. Austin, informed me that there is no known cure for prostate cancer that has metastasized outside the prostate. The best tools the world of oncology has today is to keep the cancer at bay for as long as possible, recognizing the treatments eventually will stop working and the cancer eventually will snuff out another life.

I have a good friend who has passed onto me a saying from her mother that our goal should be "to live longer that we may live longer." In other words, the longer we live, the more likely there may be new medical treatments and procedures that may extend our days. I hope for this for my diagnosis. I realize, however, that we will all eventually be called home to be with our Creator God to embark on a mysterious adventure about which we know little with certainty.

In addition to remaining on the monthly Lupron injections, the oncologist recommended I begin taking an oral medication also designed to help suppress the production of testosterone. I began taking Zytiga in late October 2019. For the next year-plus, I took four capsules of Zytiga daily plus Prednisone.

I was fortunate not to experience the negative side effects of these treatments that so many men face. Fatigue is a common side effect, but I had lots of energy. Hot flashes are another side effect, and while I got occasional hot flashes, they were mild and manageable. My blood pressure is on the low end of normal where it's been for years, and the treatments did not increase it as so often happens. The side effects impacted my immune system and red blood-cell production.

By December 2020, it was clear the Zytiga oral medication was no longer effective in controlling the PSA and cancer. My testosterone levels were still so low they couldn't be measured, but during 2020, my PSA rose from 4.26 to 16.2, a somewhat alarming increase.

In a December 2020 meeting with my oncologist, he recommended I switch from Zytiga to Xtandi. Both are hormone therapy (ADT) medications designed to suppress production of testosterone that feeds the cancer. One of the benefits of this switch is that I didn't have to take Prednisone with it. One of the side effects of Prednisone has been increased bloating and heartburn. I took the Xtandi until fall 2021, when I began chemotherapy treatments.

Another side effect of Xtandi is that it can make you less steady on your feet, and you are more prone to falling. In May 2021, while on my morning walk early one Sunday morning, when no one else was out, I tripped on the proverbial crack in the sidewalk and took an unceremonious sprawling fall. It surely would have made for a spectacular video that would have gone viral had someone been there to film my awkward tumble! My hands were scraped up and bleeding. My rib, arm, and leg were bruised. After lying on the concrete sidewalk for a few seconds taking stock of how I felt, I picked myself up and continued my walk.

While I had noticed some degree of feeling more unsteady on my feet due to the Xtandi, something I feel contributed to my fall, there was also the matter of the raised sidewalk where tree roots had pushed up the concrete, creating a trip hazard. Without Xtandi, most likely I would have been steadier on my feet and not fallen. I was fortunate that I wasn't injured more on the uncontrollable fall.

Unfortunately, the Xtandi, like the Zytiga before it, failed to control my PSA. This was a huge disappointment. I was running through the limited available treatments much faster than anyone would like and faster than what seemed normal. This worried me, and still does. For some men, ADT treatments are effective for years. They seemed to have no positive impact on me, other than the significant decrease in PSA about two months after the initial Lupron injection.

STRENGTHENING THE BONES

The words of scripture are often surprisingly relevant. From Psalm 6:2, the psalmist cries out: "Be gracious to me, O Lord, for I am languishing; O Lord, heal me, for my bones are troubled." Yes, my bones are indeed troubled as the cancer eats away at them, making the risk and severity of a fall more intense. My doctors regularly implore me to be careful and whatever I do, "Don't fall."

When I first met with my oncologist, Dr. Austin, in fall 2019, he recommended I get an infusion every three months of a medication called Zometa to help strengthen my bones. This is a necessary treatment for patients with metastatic prostate cancer that has spread to the bones.

I had my first such infusion in November 2019. The most pronounced side effect for me was a debilitating headache the next day. It took a couple of infusions to work out a helpful protocol for me that eliminated the headaches that regularly appeared the day after each infusion. My regular pattern now is to first get a saline infusion for 30 minutes, followed by a one-hour infusion of Zometa. The standard the nurses use for most patients is a 30-minute infusion of Zometa. The saline infusion followed by a slower drip of the Zometa has eliminated the headaches. I feel grateful to have discovered this solution.

Zometa is risky when tied in with major dental surgery and can result in osteonecrosis (jawbone death). This was not a factor for me until my dentist suggested the solution to a pesky and painful failed root canal was to get a tooth implant. When she informed me of this, it was almost more than I could handle emotionally on top of everything else I was dealing with. My naturopath wisely counseled me that this was simply normal age-related routine surgery.

By good fortune, I had a phone consultation with my oncologist on the morning before I was supposed to get another Zometa infusion. I mentioned to Dr. Austin that I planned to have the oral surgery to get a tooth implant and he said I should cancel the Zometa infusion for that afternoon to reduce the risk of osteonecrosis. I canceled the Zometa infusion and didn't have another one until months later after all the tooth implant work was done. Fortunately, I escaped the osteonecrosis.

While Zometa helps strengthen bones, it makes it much harder to interpret the results of bone scans that are used to assess the progression or regression of cancerous lesions. The Zometa shows up on scans as growth and it is next to impossible to distinguish between cancerous growth and Zometa build-up.

SPIRALING EFFECTS OF PAIN

In early July 2021, with my PSA at 28.2 (up from 17.8 in January 2021), I began to experience sudden, intense pain that interrupted my sleep and impacted my ability to exist without excruciating pain in my tailbone area. My body involuntarily jerked me around from the pain. There was no pain-free position, and the pain came on rapidly, a day and night difference. Going on my normal daily walks was out of the question for about three weeks. My naturopath informed me this sudden onset of pain for cancer patients was common. The pain was and is a troubling reminder that my time in this life is limited. Fortunately, my wife moved back to Seattle from Boise at this time (just prior to my son and his family returning to Seattle) and was available to help me manage the pain.

To control the pain, I was advised by my oncologist to take Norco, a narcotic pain reliever. I started taking it on July 22. It helped control the pain, but as often occurs with medications such as this, severe constipation and urinary retention set in. That brought its own level of pain. The doctor hadn't told me this was a likely side effect of Norco. Pain-management nurses worked with me how to manage the pain and reduce the constipation.

On Aug. 10, I was bloated and in pain and hadn't urinated or had a bowel movement for days. I called the consulting nurse who advised me to go to urgent care immediately to be outfitted with a catheter. I was emotionally exhausted and fragile and didn't want to spend my Tuesday evening at the hospital. My wife, Catherine, took charge, loaded me into the car, and off we went. Without her presence and action, I don't know what would have happened to me.

The draining of my bladder and the installation of a catheter were incredibly painful experiences. I had the catheter for almost three months. On October 1, I went to urgent care yet again when the catheter failed, and a nurse put a new one in place. When I had the catheter, it was painful and difficult to move without exacerbating the pain.

On November 2, I went in for a routine check to see if the catheter could be removed. Things had stabilized enough, I was able to urinate without the catheter, and they removed it. The freedom felt wonderful.

However, the medical staff who removed the catheter were concerned about swelling in my left leg, to which the catheter bag had been strapped. They immediately sent me to urgent care for an ultrasound that revealed blood clots had formed up and down my left leg. Whether the clots developed solely because of my catheter-induced inactivity due to pain and discomfort of the catheter, or also because of the cancer, I don't know. Regardless, I was put on blood-thinner medication and told I would be taking it for the rest of my life—however long that may be.

The fall of 2021 was a miserable and painful time, and many of the details are blurry for me now. Perhaps I just don't want to remember the pain and discomfort of those days. I certainly don't want to ever repeat that experience, even though I know that may be in my future given the nature of metastatic prostate cancer.

RADIATING THE ROGUE CELLS

On Aug. 9, 2021, my PSA skyrocketed to 59.0, surely a sign, along with the pain, that the cancer was on the move in an aggressive way.

On Aug. 18, I began the first of 10 targeted radiation treatments designed to zap the growth of the cancerous cells and provide me with much-needed relief to function daily.

At the first targeted radiation treatment, I was in such excruciating pain I needed help from the kind radiation staff to lie on the radiation table and had to rely on them to help me sit up at the end of the treatment. The treatment was about an hour long, during which I had to lie perfectly still on a rock-hard table while they drew lines on my body, mapped out how the radiation machine would target the cancer, and zapped me. I was in agony.

Fortunately, the remaining nine treatments were each only about 15 minutes long, if that. As the treatments continued, I began to experience pain relief and I found I could get on and off the table by myself. By Aug. 31, I had completed the course of treatment. The pain had significantly subsided.

Nevertheless, when I had blood tests on Sept. 9, my PSA had inched upward yet again, from 59.0 a month previously to 61.6. I was told the positive impacts of radiation would continue for weeks if not months after the final treatment.

The radiation eventually knocked the cancerous cells back and eliminated the pain, reducing it to mild discomfort. Curiously, my oncologist had told me my PSA would not go down after targeted radiation. However, on Oct. 8, my PSA dropped 58%, from 61.6 in early September to 25.9.

I later had a conversation with the radiation doctor who told me if the targeted radiation focused on the only or main area of the lesions, then he would expect the PSA to drop. If, however, he noted, there were multiple areas of cancerous activity and the radiation targeted only one of those areas, he wouldn't expect much, if any, decrease in PSA. His explanation made a lot of sense to me, and I wished then that the radiation and oncology doctors talked more with one another to have a more complete picture.

It was one more reminder to me that I was the general contractor in managing various specialty medical professionals, each who brought a narrow expertise but didn't necessarily have broad experience to understand the impacts of other treatments.

The main negative side effect I experienced from the targeted radiation was fatigue, which lingered for many months. I remember in the months after the targeted radiation being out of breath and unable to do more than an old-man shuffle on my now short morning walks. I also needed to sleep for hours on end during the day. Fatigue impacts much more than the body and I found myself emotionally fragile (see later chapter).

KILLING THE CANCER CELLS

When I completed the targeted radiation and with the success of lowering my PSA, I thought I would get a reprieve from additional treatments for a while. My oncologist strongly recommended chemotherapy (Docetaxel). He argued that we needed to be aggressive in keeping the cancer at bay. So, on Oct. 25, 2021, I went in for my first chemo treatment.

Starting chemo felt like a death sentence and the beginning of the end of the road for me. In one sense, that's true. Chemo is just another step on the journey that will eventually bring me closer to my Maker and the end of this earthly journey. I have had an unrealistic expectation that somehow some treatment would solve everything, and everything would be back to normal. Instead, I need to remind myself that this is an uncertain journey, and I will be subjected to more tests and treatments. Certainly, I can hope that the treatments will result in a respite from pain and a slowing of the cancer. But I don't know.

For the first six chemo treatments, which were spaced out at three-week intervals, I was hit with extreme fatigue about two to three days after the chemo that lasted for three to four days. During the fatigue times, I was very emotional and ended up sleeping or lying on the couch for at least two of those days, completely immobilized by the treatments. Maybe the fatigue was the result of my body not being used to the chemo, the residual effect of the radiation fatigue, or the relaxing impacts of cannabis that I started taking in fall 2020 for its anti-cancer properties.

Starting with the seventh chemo treatment in late February 2022, I mercifully escaped the extreme fatigue. Interestingly, at the same time, I stopped taking cannabis due to brain fog, so perhaps that was a major contributing factor to the fatigue. As I continued with chemo, by the 10th session, I was starting to feel run down as my red-blood counts continued to go down, along with my iron levels. In early May 2022, I began taking iron supplements recommended by my naturopath. Within a little over a week, I began to feel a bit more energy. Three months after starting the iron supplements, blood tests showed my iron levels were within the normal ranges.

When I began chemo (or what one of my chemo nurses called "healing juice"), I was informed that nausea was one of the side effects I might experience. I was apprehensive, but I feel grateful that, by and large, I have escaped this unpleasantry. There have been times when I felt I might be nearing nausea, but I never vomited. That didn't stop me from keeping an emergency bowl by my bed just in case. There were a few times I reached for the bowl in the middle of the night but never vomited. It was more an experience of acid reflux that caused me to wake up and feel uncomfortable.

I was also informed that neuropathy was also a potential side effect of chemo. Neuropathy occurs when the fingers and toes slowly lose the sensation to feel. This also was a big fear of mine in approaching chemo. I didn't want anything to interfere with my quality of life, but I did want to live, so I realized I needed to deal with the risks.

I never experienced neuropathy in my fingers although at times it felt like it was perhaps beginning to develop. My toes were another story. After about three or four months of chemo, my toes began to lose sensation. It was mild. I began taking a supplement from my naturopath designed to restore nerve damage. I also began to put my feet and hands in ice just prior to and during the chemo infusions. I wore compression socks. Finally, my experience convinces me that the cumulative impact of acupuncture to help prevent neuropathy has had beneficial impacts.

One of the side effects of chemo is hair loss. The nurse at my first chemo session told me that in three weeks when I was to return for the next chemo treatment, I wouldn't have any hair. The hair on my head and my beard began to thin out, but the hair loss eventually stopped, and my hair began to grow again. For a while, it grew thick. It also came in curly on my right side, unlike my normal straight hair. My hair also has turned totally white. My beard has thinned and turned whiter but it's still there. Hair on my arms, legs, and chest did fall. In the grand scheme of things, losing hair is a minor thing. I simply want to stay alive for as long as possible and live well in the process.

In mid-August 2022, after nine months of chemo, my hair started falling out and thinning again. I also began to experience more fatigue after my 14th chemo session. I would gladly take the hair loss and fatigue if only the cancerous cells would disappear.

On Sept. 6, 2022, after 10 months of chemo treatments with Docetaxel, I had my 15th chemo treatment and my first one with a different chemo drug, Cabazitaxel. As of mid-November 2022, my PSA began slowing inching down although it was still well above normal at 35.6. The pain and discomfort in my sacrum and hips melted away shortly after I began the Cabazitaxel. Fatigue was a side effect of this chemo. The jury is still out on how long the Cabazitaxel will have beneficial impacts in controlling the cancer.

SWITCHING ONCOLOGISTS

In spring 2020, Dr. Austin suggested I obtain a second opinion about my cancer treatment from another Seattle medical center. Given everything at stake and my less-than-full confidence in him, I told him I would like to do that. I met with Dr. Craig for the second opinion assessment.

She had obviously done her homework reviewing my file. She was matter of fact, a good communicator, and knowledgeable about treatment options. She confirmed that the treatment I was on with the testosterone-blocking medication was the right course of action for now. It was, however, somewhat depressing for me in that she reminded me that the statistical clock for the progression of the cancer was ticking.

At the same time, she suggested I sign up for genetic testing to assess whether I had any mutations more likely to cause prostate cancer. I went through the testing and the results were negative with respect to prostate cancer. However, the testing did identify two mutations that would make me more susceptible to colorectal cancer by the time I reached my 80s. With the likelihood of me living that long relatively low given the nature of metastatic prostate cancer, I have chosen not to pursue some of the other tests recommended. There's only so much I can handle emotionally. Plus, I don't want to spend all my time at medical appointments. There are still things I want to do and feel called to.

In fall 2019, prior to the second-opinion appointment with Dr. Craig, I had asked Dr. Austin whether I should get a baseline bone density test given the negative impacts of Zytiga on my bones. He said that such a test was not necessary. I was surprised but accepted his judgment. When I met with Dr. Craig, I asked the same question. She strongly advised I should get a bone-density test.

In mid-April 2020, when I met again with Dr. Austin, I relayed to him Dr. Craig's recommendation. Dr. Austin said getting a bone density test made sense to him, a complete reversal of his previous response to me from him six months prior that had not been accompanied by any rationale why such a test was not necessary. I was quickly losing confidence in Dr. Austin's opinions without supporting reasons.

The different answers to questions between doctors and the inconsistencies even with one doctor make it a challenge to always be on my toes about my treatment, especially when this is such an emotional journey.

During the time Dr. Austin was my oncologist, he seemed to become exasperated that I wasn't deferentially accepting everything he said. My philosophy has been that this is my body and my life, and I want to make the wisest decisions possible about my treatment. Furthermore, I wanted to unpack some of the unknowns about future treatments to reduce my increasing anxiety. I got only generalized and non-specific answers and began to wonder whether he really had much depth of knowledge. Of course, I realize that more information is a double-edged sword for me, and that more information also can be quite scary.

My relationship with Dr. Austin remained cordial, or so I thought, even if the content lacked specificity. I made the decision to switch to a different oncologist on the day I met with him for my first chemotherapy treatment in late October 2021. I was scared, perhaps in large measure because I didn't have much information about what chemo would entail or what potential side effects might be. We often respond in fear to unknown situations. I had done some reading on chemo treatments, but neither Dr. Austin nor any other of the medical staff had provided me with any advanced education about what to expect.

As we spoke on that day just prior to my first chemo treatment, I said the following to Dr. Austin: "I know it's above your pay grade, but it would be nice if the hospital provided advanced education for chemo patients." It seemed like a very reasonable thing for me to say. I framed my words in a way that didn't place responsibility on him for the lack of such education. My tone of voice was calm and respectful. I had been talking with a good friend from college who had begun chemo treatments a week before me, and she benefited from a significant education program run by her hospital.

I was flabbergasted by Dr. Austin's response to my comment. He replied by saying "I sense you're being more adversarial than usual." First, I was not being adversarial in any manner. Being adversarial is not part of my personality. Second, his comment that he thought I was normally adversarial revealed a lot about him and that he was not comfortable with a patient asking any questions or making any comments. His insecurity drove him to do everything possible to keep the patient in the dark with vague comments and him in control.

My wife, Catherine, was with me at that first pre-chemo appointment with Dr. Austin. She responded to the doctor's "adversarial" comment by saying that chemo was a scary treatment option, and more information would be better.

I resolved then and there that Dr. Austin was not a good match for me. I relayed the content of this "adversarial" conversation to friends who strongly urged me to change doctors. I didn't, however, want to jump from the frying pan into the fire, so I approached the change slowly and methodically.

At the end of 2021, Dr. Austin was on vacation when it was time to meet with an oncologist for approval to proceed with my fourth chemo treatment. Dr. Percy was assigned to meet with me. She was a pleasant doctor who provided more specific information in our short meeting than I had ever received from Dr. Austin in the two years I had been under his care. The contrast between their styles and knowledge was astounding.

I decided I would wait, however, before formally making the shift in oncologists until I met yet a different oncologist for my mid-January 2022 chemo appointment, at which neither Dr. Austin nor Dr. Percy would be available. While I was fully satisfied with Dr. Percy, I wanted to have as much information as possible before making the formal switch to a differ-ent oncologist.

I met with Dr. Dravus on Jan. 18. While he seemed pleasant and knowledgeable, he was not nearly as effective a communicator as Dr. Percy, and his answers to my questions were not as clear or as expansive as those of Dr. Percy. I was a bit unnerved that Dr. Dravus turned his head away from me when he was speaking. He failed to discuss with me things he put on the after-visit summary as things we had supposedly discussed. His listening to my lungs with his stethoscope was perfunctory and way too fast to be able to notice anything or to even give me a chance to take a deep breath.

Shortly after meeting with Dr. Dravus, I called the hospital and made the formal change of my oncologist from Dr. Austin to Dr. Percy. I had enough information to know that Dr. Percy was the best fit for me. I have been quite pleased by continuing to work with her.

If I ever had any remaining questions whether choosing Dr. Percy over Dr. Dravus was the right decision, my initial concerns about Dr. Dravus were confirmed in a later appointment I had with him when Dr. Percy was not available. At that appointment, Dr. Dravus ordered a chromogranin-A blood test for me.

The result came back significantly elevated, most likely because he had not notified me that I should stop taking Omeprazole to deal with heartburn caused by Prednisone. Omeprazole is listed on my medical records as a medication I take regularly, and it is known to cause spiked results. When I later met with Dr. Percy to discuss the result, she was diplomatic but confused by why Dr. Dravus had ordered this test since my CT and bone scans from March 2022 didn't reflect anything that would be of concern. When I met with my naturopathic doctor later, she was blunter about how it was inadvisable for Dr. Dravus to have ordered the blood test.

I realized I had made a good decision in switching my oncology care to Dr. Percy and not Dr. Dravus. It also made me realize that doctors don't have all the answers and are different just as all people are different. Somehow, I expected I would get the same level of treatment from any oncologist. Treating metastatic prostate cancer, perhaps like many other diseases, appears to be as much an art as a science.

SCANNING THE HORIZON

In mid-August 2022, my PSA continued its relentless rise, going from 23.1 to 27.6. By early September, the PSA went up marginally to 28.1, bringing momentary hope. Overall, the trend is upward and not promising.

My oncologist ordered another CT and bone scan to get a sense for how much the cancer has grown. The results showed new areas of growth that hadn't shown up on previous scans from March 2022. In mid-September, I had a PET scan. It showed in greater detail the spread of the cancer. I am on the waiting list for a new treatment approved by the FDA in March 2022, called Lutetium-177-PSMA that delivers radiation by infusion directly to just the cancerous cells. I will start that when it is determined the latest chemotherapy medication, Cabazitaxel, has failed.

CHAPTER 7

ALTERNATIVE TREATMENTS

The natural healing force within each one of us
is the greatest force in getting well.

Hippocrates

Early on, I resolved that I wanted to do everything possible for my health and give myself the best possible chance of extending my days. I didn't want to second-guess myself and wonder whether I should have pursued some different treatment. I have done so much to promote my health and keep the cancer at bay with traditional and alternative treatments. I don't want to have regrets about how I have managed my health. Thus, I have been open to trying new things that otherwise I might have considered outside of my comfort zone.

In other words, what do I have to lose?

While I do everything I can for my health, I realize this is a partnership with God, and he is sovereign. He is the one who ordains how long I will live, so when I transition out of this life, I can rest assured that it is his will, and the timing is right. This isn't to suggest that leaving this life early makes me comfortable. Far from it. I have so much more I want to contribute and experience. There are people to love and books to write.

Nevertheless, I will trust God with the length of my days while doing what I can to extend them. It's an awkward tension.

Writing this three and a half years since I was diagnosed, I increasingly feel that the cancer remains on the move, deepening the question of how long this body will last. Certainly, part of me can feel like the alternative treatments haven't worked, especially if I define "worked" as a cure. It's an open question whether the alternative treatments have extended my life. I do think, however, they have helped me to manage the rigors of hormone therapy, radiation, and chemotherapy better than other men faced with the same disease. The alternative treatments also have extended my ability to remain functional.

Each alternative treatment brings a rich tradition, often extending back for millennia and addressing how the body works and what can be done to make it healthy. Each one can serve as a healthy complement to traditional and limited Western medicine.

NUTRITIONIST

Soon after I was diagnosed, I decided that changing my eating habits couldn't hurt and might be beneficial. I have always tried to eat well and take care of myself, but I wanted to do everything possible to give myself the best chance at keeping the cancer at bay for as long as possible.

While I knew there is no cure for metastatic prostate cancer, I needed to live with some form of hope. I felt that taking actions that might have healing benefit would be therapeutic. Perhaps I was still in denial about the reality of cancer attacking my body when I was still in my prime and hoping to contribute so much more to this world.

Evidence exists that a plant-based diet can help slow cancer.[14] I engaged the services of a nutritionist to guide me, and Michelle was helpful. Initially, I met with her in her office until the pandemic forced our meetings into a virtual space.

For about two years, mainly during the height of the pandemic, I religiously ate a plant-based diet with no animal protein (meat, dairy, eggs) or sugar. I created a spreadsheet with the items I was eating and the protein value of each. When I shared the content of my vegan diet with my naturopath, she exclaimed it was "freaking awesome!" That made me feel that I was on the right track.

I have read conflicting information about the benefits and risks of salmon. Some information noted salmon was good for dealing with prostate cancer, while other information suggested that any animal protein, and especially salmon, could exacerbate the cancer. At first, I ate salmon, then dropped it, then added it back into my diet.

When I began chemotherapy in fall 2021, I realized that my red and white blood counts were being decimated and that I needed to have a more robust diet to keep myself healthy. Thus, I added meats back into my diet for protein. I even began to occasionally eat red meat, something I hadn't done since college, save for maybe a half-dozen times to be polite in social settings.

I have read that intermittent fasting may help prevent and deal with cancer. Consequently, I have maintained a schedule in which my goal is to finish dinner by 6 p.m. and not eat again until breakfast around 8 a.m., giving me 14 hours of an intermittent fast.

Likewise, there is information that juicing, a process that extracts juice from fresh fruits and vegetables, may reduce cancer risk and boost one's immune system. The thought of buying a large quantity of fresh produce, cleaning it, and running it through a special machine seemed overwhelming. But I found a local company that sold and delivered such juices. I signed up for it and drank them until the company changed its business model and stopped home delivery.

Developing and changing my diet and cooking for myself during the first year and a half of the pandemic was fulfilling. I can't directly correlate my health in this season of cancer with my new diet, but it certainly didn't hurt, and it may have been beneficial.

NATUROPATHIC DOCTOR

Early on, I was having one of my monthly lunches with Frank, a good friend of many years, at our favorite Mexican restaurant in Seattle. He said that he had been seeing a naturopathic doctor to help him with a variety of health issues. I knew little about naturopaths and had only a vaguely negative impression of them, but in keeping with my growing resolve to bring as many resources as possible to bear on my health, I made an appointment to see his naturopath, Dr. Ives.

She was full of energy, a bullet-speed talker, who offered immediate advice, but didn't interact seriously with my questions. I was concerned she didn't take the time to understand my situation and didn't articulate her statements in words or concepts that made sense to me. I sensed her suggested protocols didn't seem particularly tailored to metastatic prostate cancer but instead were generic suggestions she provided to all her patients.

She ordered a comprehensive blood and urine test to assess deficiencies I might have. I met with her twice, including a session to review the results of the lab work, before realizing this was not a good match, and I lacked confidence in her.

This was a disappointing introduction that only reinforced my stereotype of naturopathic doctors as a bit outside the norm of reason. I resolved, however, not to give up hope.

I still wanted to approach my health holistically. Online research led me to understand that a whole field of naturopaths focused on cancer patients, a discipline sometimes referred to as integrative oncology. One broad definition of integrative oncology calls it:

…a patient-centered, evidence-informed field of cancer care that utilizes mind and body practices, natural products, and/or lifestyle modifications from different traditions alongside conventional cancer treatments. Integrative oncology aims to optimize health, quality of life, and clinical outcomes across the cancer care continuum and to empower people to prevent cancer and become active participants before, during, and beyond cancer treatment.[15]

With this understanding, I began to research whether any naturopathic doctors in Seattle focused on cancer patients. One doctor seemed to have the credentials and experience I was looking for. I met with Dr. Buckle in mid-February 2020, just before COVID-19 shut down the world. I was impressed with her knowledge, her matter of fact and yet warm communication style, and her experience with cancer. I have continued to meet with her virtually since then. The fact that she laughs at my jokes is also a plus!

I have found her to be incredibly knowledgeable, and she has solved several problems for me with her recommendations. She understands well the world of oncology and has many tools that traditional doctors don't have. I have no doubt her guidance is one of the reasons I have done as well as I have with managing side-effects from my treatments.

Over time, as issues have arisen, Dr. Buckle has recommended supplements to take. I take more than 30 supplements daily, almost a full meal! I also have taken other supplements for a short period of time until a specific condition was resolved.

I take supplements recommended by Dr. Buckle to support the following:

- Immune system
- Bone health
- Healthy bone marrow
- Gastrointestinal (GI) health

- Help coat and soothe the esophagus and prevent heartburn
- Cardiac function
- Liver function
- Healthy digestion
- Improve fat digestion and firm up stool
- Reduce reflux symptoms
- Help reduce PSA
- Reduce urinary symptoms
- Help prevent neuropathy and support energy
- Support white and red blood cell production
- Support anti-oxidation
- Help reduce clotting
- Support iron deficiency
- Support vascular integrity
- Reduce edema

Some supplements also have anti-cancer and anti-inflammatory properties and help suppress tumors.

Naturopathic advice also was helpful in how I dealt with my traditional doctors. For instance, in late October 2019, my oncologist prescribed an oral medication (Zytiga) designed to suppress the production of testosterone. Testosterone is a major source of food for prostate cancer. One side effect of Zytiga is that it can damage the liver as reflected in liver enzymes that can be elevated to unhealthy levels. Predictably, my liver enzymes (AST and ALT) began to rise. After a little more than two months on the medication, these levels were outside the normal range. After two months more, my AST and ALT levels had spiked to unhealthy levels. My oncologist, Dr. Austin, was concerned but wasn't ready to reduce my dosage of Zytiga (his only solution) until the levels were even higher.

I expressed my concern about the alarming rise of the liver enzymes to Dr. Buckle. She had a ready answer: I should begin taking a curcumin supplement. I followed her instructions. The results were nearly miraculous. Six weeks after I began the supplement, my ALT had dropped from a high of 242 (normal range is 5 to 50) down to 36. Similarly, my AST had dropped from a high of 106 (normal range is 6 to 35) to 29. Since then, these blood-test indicators of the health of my liver have remained solidly within the normal range despite the expected side effects of Zytiga and other medications.

Sadly, my oncologist, Dr. Austin, never expressed curiosity about or interest in what had caused the dramatic drop of the liver enzymes. I mentioned to him the curcumin supplement, and his only comment was to advise me not to take any supplements at all because no studies support their potential efficacy.

When I relayed his comment to Dr. Buckle, she assured me that such studies exist but that oncologists don't read those studies. Unfortunately, our medical system is partitioned into silos, with no one discipline having a complete picture.

It's amazing how wonderfully God has created our bodies, and often things can be done to bring things into balance.

After about three months of chemotherapy, I noticed my stool was becoming loose but was not diarrhea. I mentioned this to Dr. Buckle during a meeting in early February 2022. She immediately suggested I increase the dosage of the pancreatic enzyme I was taking with my lunch and instead take the supplement before each of my three meals. I followed her instructions, and the result was an immediate firming up of my stool.

After I started the Cabazitaxel chemotherapy in September 2022, I began to experience heartburn, coughing, semi-nausea, and other uncomfortable gastrointestinal tract issues. Dr. Buckle suggested I begin taking some additional supplements. Within a few days, my symptoms cleared up.

Dr. Buckle also recommended I begin to take Artemisinin as a natural form of chemotherapy before each of my weekend meals. I don't know whether this supplement has contributed to helping slow the growth of the rogue cells.

To address swelling on my right foot, Dr. Buckle recommended I begin a regimen of Contrast Hydrotherapy. This involved soaking my feet and legs in warm water for three minutes, then putting them in ice cold water for 30 seconds. I repeated this cycle three times, three times a day. I stopped this practice in summer 2021 when the sacrum pain became unbearable.

Based on recommendations by two friends, I also have had two appointments with a different naturopath as a second-opinion reality check. I want to bring as many resources as I can to maintaining my health for as long as possible, but I remain indebted to Dr. Buckle, with whom I continue to meet monthly.

ACUPUNCTURIST

As I continued to explore alternative treatments, I mentioned acupuncture to Dr. Buckle who agreed it could have beneficial impacts, including reducing the severity of hot flashes caused by hormone medication to suppress testosterone production. Acupuncture, we agreed, also might help manage pain. My naturopath recommended an acupuncturist who works in her suite of medical professionals.

I began acupuncture treatments at the end of May 2020 just as the world began to slowly and cautiously open up after a near shutdown due to COVID-19. I have continued with acupuncture treatments almost every week since then. With my compromised immune system, I risked exposure to Covid, but the risk seemed worth taking. Laura, my acupuncturist, has been cautious and has implemented safety protocols, including that no other person is in the office suite during my visits. She always wears a mask and a plastic face shield, and I always wear an N-95 mask. She takes my temperature every Sunday afternoon when I come in for treatment and meticulously cleans surfaces between patients.

Every week, Laura asks me about my stress levels and emotions. She is concerned about how stress is impacting me physically, and her treatments always address this.

Over time, her treatments also have focused on pains I have felt in my right rib and sacrum, locations where the cancer has spread. She also has addressed ongoing tightness in my left shoulder and a swollen right foot. The pain in my right rib was particularly uncomfortable and impacted my sleep. That discomfort went away over time although it has slowly begun to re-emerge. Laura's work on my right foot reduced its swelling. Curiously, swelling has begun in my left leg and foot, likely the result of the cancer and chemotherapy treatments.

Perhaps most important, as I began chemotherapy, the acupuncture treatments have focused on preventing neuropathy in my toes and fingers. While I have felt mild neuropathy in my toes, I never have experienced it in my fingers. Certainly, this preventive work has helped, as has taking a supplement to revitalize nerves, and icing my fingers and toes just prior to and during chemotherapy infusions to dull the nerve endings.

When I mentioned to Laura, I was feeling heartburn, she placed needles in my chest. Within a minute, I began to experience relief. Likewise, when my left hip was hurting, she strategically placed needles and it brought instantaneous but not complete relief.

Finally, Laura listens empathetically and has provided other excellent health suggestions, including constant and gentle reminders to hydrate adequately and to practice stretches that complement the acupuncture.

She is an important part of my medical team. Regular acupuncture treatments have helped me manage pain and reduced side effects of cancer treatments.

OTHER TREATMENTS

During this journey, I have had a variety of other treatments. I stopped most of these in summer 2021 when pain from my spiking PSA became so intense that I couldn't accomplish much of anything. These treatments include:

- I have seen a chiropractor to address left shoulder tightness and discomfort in moving my head to the left. These treatments were effective and improved my posture.

- I have seen a friend who is a massage therapist. My initial thought was that this seemed like a mere luxury. But as I talked with friends and read more about it, I realized it could improve my immune system and stimulate my white blood count, for which I needed help.

- Upon the recommendation of Dr. Buckle, I had about five months of twice weekly treatments of high-dose IV Vitamin C treatments with the hope it might help control the cancer.

- I also received weekly Hyperbaric Oxygen Treatments (HBOT) for about five months. According to the FDA, "HBOT involves breathing 100% (pure) oxygen while in a special space called a hyperbaric chamber. The air pressure inside is raised to a level that is higher than normal air pressure. The increased air pressure in the chamber helps the lungs collect more oxygen."[16] This treatment is designed to make it harder for cancer cells to thrive in such an oxygen-rich environment.

CHAPTER 8

ADVOCACY

I learned a long time ago the wisest thing I can do
is be on my own side,
be an advocate for myself and others like me.

Maya Angelou

All of us, in varying degrees want to be "taken care of," and I feel no differently.

I want experts to guide me, solve my problems, and reassure me with comforting answers based on years of experience and knowledge. One of my surprising and disconcerting discoveries that dawned on me at the beginning of this journey was that no one member of my medical team had all the answers. In fact, I realized they sometimes had no answers or different answers. How could I handle conflicting advice? How could I manage gaps of knowledge? Who would make final decisions?

Surely, I reasoned, since I was not the first man to be diagnosed with metastatic prostate cancer, the medical world must have established a treatment protocol. In one sense, this is true.[17] But in another sense, I soon entered the Wild West, where my job became to take charge of my treatment and serve as my strongest advocate.

I have a strong desire and will to live fully and faithfully for however many days God grants to me. There are things I still feel called to. Thus, I decided to do everything I could to manage my health with the best and widest range of advice. Consequently, I communicated with friends, read a lot, and consulted with a variety of traditional and alternative medical professionals, culling the best from all approaches.

I always can do more research, but I have only so much time and emotional bandwidth. While I want to be responsible for managing my health, I also don't want it to consume all my minutes. I have tried to maintain a delicate balance between researching information about cancer treatment and living life fully.

Western medicine has its strengths. It has helped keep me alive with treatments that suppress the production of testosterone (the main food for prostate cancer), and its targeted radiation and chemotherapy are designed to shrink and kill cancer cells. But its approach does not recognize other things that can promote health.

Unfortunately, Western medicine often dismisses other approaches, and generally maintains such opinions without evidence. If I want to stay alive and thrive, I must explore all potential solutions, since neither Western medicine nor alternative treatments has all the answers. Each offers valuable perspectives but neither has the complete picture.

I realize that metastatic prostate cancer has no cure, but I also reason that I can take steps to extend my days and promote a good quality of life.

At one meeting with Dr. Buckle, I bemoaned the dysfunctional and fragmented world of traditional medicine. She wisely and graciously calmed me by stating that Western doctors simply do what they are trained to do, and she does what she is trained to do. Her comment helped me to recognize more fully that it is up to me and my assembled team to figure out the best steps for me. Fortunately, Dr. Buckle is an oncology naturopath, so she understands both the world of traditional oncology and the natural medical tools that Western doctors consider foreign.

In summer 2020, Dr. Buckle, asked me to discuss with Dr. Austin, my oncologist, four tests that she recommended: a PET scan, a circulating tumor cells blood test, and ESR and CRP blood tests to measure inflammation.

Dr. Austin refused to authorize these tests, stating that none of the results would change his treatment plan for me. However, Dr. Buckle noted that the results might change her own treatment plan for me. It was yet another example of siloed medical options between traditional and alternative approaches and reinforced that I need to be my own advocate.

Dr. Austin suggested that I obtain a second opinion about the tests, and I chose to get one through a different hospital. When I met with Dr. Smith, the second opinion oncologist, he also refused to authorize the tests. His words dripped with contempt, cynicism, and negativity about naturopaths. This unpleasant experience left a sour taste in my mouth.

Medical school apparently doesn't teach would-be doctors much about bedside manner. Or any training they might receive may not be effective. What is most important is the comfort that doctors have with themselves and their ability to interact with patients. Some doctors appear afraid of embracing new concepts and more interested in control based on their visions of reality. This sad situation adds to the emotional challenges faced by patients.

I returned to Dr. Buckle, who ordered the inflammation-related blood tests, and I took her order to my health-care provider when I obtained my next routine bank of blood tests. My medical plan covers such additional blood tests. Fortunately, the ESR and CRP test results showed extremely low inflammation. This made me wonder why my oncologist wasn't willing to obtain such information and cooperate with me as I worked with him and Dr. Buckle. I also wondered whether financial considerations entered his thoughts.

Sometimes the culprit presents itself as bureaucracy. In August 2022, my current oncologist, Dr. Percy, ordered a PET scan that would indicate whether my body likely would likely respond to a Lutetium-177-PSMA treatment. My medical provider doesn't provide this type of PET scan, so I was referred to a different hospital. After my doctor sent the referral, I called the other hospital to make an appointment. The hospital said it could not find the referral and would have to go through a stack of faxes. I said it was important to get it scheduled quickly as the cancer was growing in me. I offered to email the referral, bring it by, or talk with a manager. I called the next day and got a similar answer with the promise of a call-back. After I received no call-back, I called the next day. The person on the phone immediately knew who I was. I said that I intended to be politely persistent. I was informed a radiologist was reviewing the referral and would call me back in an hour or two. When I didn't hear back after two hours, I called again and got the appointment scheduled. Had I waited, the delay could have extended for weeks.

This journey has taught me that I need serve as general contractor, responsible for coordinating various medical specialties and trying to make it all work seamlessly and cohesively. This was a big surprise, as I had thought that's what doctors were supposed to do. Some hospitals wisely assign nurse navigators to help coordinate treatments and advocate for the patient. My health-care provider has nurse navigators for other forms of cancer but not for prostate cancer.

Certainly, not everyone responds in the same way I have. Dealing with one's failing health can be an intensely emotional experience, and sometimes we don't possess the bandwidth to serve as our own advocate and general contractor. To cope, it can feel easier to sit back and allow medical professionals to dictate our treatment.

No single answer fits everyone. We each must forge our path given the nature of our illness, our financial resources, and our emotional support.

Because I had been blessed to enjoy excellent health, I lacked experience in navigating the complexities of medical treatments. I thought, or hoped, that doctors would tell me exactly what to do and that I would feel confident in their advice. I didn't expect to be so active in managing my treatment. It took me a while to figure out that I needed to be my own strongest advocate and that no one else would, or could, make the right health-care decisions for me.

CHAPTER 9

CO-HEALING

Healing is a partnership with God.

Mike Purdy

Early in my journey through these uncharted waters, I resolved that I didn't want to have regrets about whether I had done everything possible to promote my health, healing, and longevity. When my Creator calls me home from this earthly pilgrimage, it will be the right timing in his economy. I will not pass from this earth until I have finished the work to which God has called me. Our gracious and loving Father numbers my days.

While I know this intellectually, I worry every day that my life will be cut short. My worry relates to my expectations and hopes for the number of my days. Certainly, however, God's purposes will not be thwarted by my passage to the next grand adventure, whenever and whatever that may be.

I have a dear friend who, at age nine, survived the crash of a small airplane that tragically ended her father's life. Her father piloted that ill-fated flight, and the cause of the accident was likely his error. Though my friend professes no belief in God, she is one of the most astute theologians I know. She reminds me that I need not fear the date of my death and that it will occur when the time is right, and not before.

However, a natural and uncomfortable tension exists between being proactive about my health and trusting in God's sovereignty. Is it wrong for me to pursue things that may promote health and healing in the hope of extending my days instead of sitting back in recognition that God's perfect timing will override my feeble attempts? Another way to express this age-old conundrum is whether God's sovereignty or human free will ultimately drives the course of human events.

Ultimately, God is the healer. This is true whether healing comes because of my actions, medical intervention, the natural healing that is woven into creation, or miraculous healing. So, I work for my healing in partnership with God to honor his good creation regardless of how many days my Creator has ordained for me.

If working toward healing honors God's creation, what should be my role? The answer may lie in a concept I would describe as co-healing.

For example, when a new baby is born, who created the new life? A new birth is a miracle of God's creation, and we understand little about how this new body and soul came into being. However, the parents actively worked with God to create this new life. The new life is a partnership between God and the parents. Thus, we might say that new birth is an action of co-creation.

In the context of healing, we are co-healers with God. He ultimately brings about healing, and he often works in and through our efforts.

CHAPTER 10

PAIN

Pain insists upon being attended to.
God whispers to us in our pleasures, speaks in our consciences,
but shouts in our pains.
It is his megaphone to rouse a deaf world.

C.S. Lewis

I don't like pain. None of us does. Mercifully, for most of the time since I was diagnosed with metastatic prostate cancer, I have not experienced intense pain. The summer and early fall of 2021 were an exception when the cancerous cells ramped up their relentless activity and left me literally writhing in pain. The pain finally ceased when the cancerous cells shrunk under the influence of targeted radiation.

I am under no illusion that, short of a miraculous healing or new treatments that may cure metastatic prostate cancer, my future will likely include more excruciating pain. I don't look forward to that, but pain often accompanies our passage from this world to the next.

In the words of the song "Because He Lives" by Bill Gaither, "And then one day, I'll cross the river. I'll fight life's final war with pain." How will I respond to other bouts of pain? I hope I will do so with grace and a recognition that it is part of life, but it won't be fun.

Physical pain has sapped me of my ability to think clearly, creating what I call a brain fog. That was difficult because the life of the mind has always been so invigorating for me. It obliterated my emotional energy since all my limited energies were devoted to simply trying to reduce the pain. I felt as if my mind could not function, and my emotions were raw. Pain separated me from thinking and feeling. Spirituality gave way to mere existence. In the words of one wise friend, "Pain can be an octopus, with various arms of agony squeezing the body and psyche."[18]

Although it provides small consolation while we endure pain, we know that it is not for eternity, that it is temporary while we live on this earth.

My counselor, Alyssa, reminded me that God knows what pain feels like, and that Jesus felt excruciating pain—the painful and humiliating agony of death on a cross. With his hands and feet brutally pierced by nails as he hung on a wooden Roman cross, the weight of his body ripped at his flesh.

Even in the midst of our pain, God doesn't withdraw from us, though it feels like he has withdrawn since we don't feel his presence then. Is it possible for me to remember to pray that I might experience God's presence when I feel pain?

Not feeling God's presence when pain strikes is part of our humanity. I am reminded of Jesus' words as he hung on the cross. Jesus, who was, in a mysterious and unexplainable way, both fully human and fully God, cried out as nails pierced his flesh, "My God, my God, why hast thou forsaken me?" (Matthew 27:46). He felt abandoned. Pain had so overwhelmed his body that he was unable to think clearly. Pain does that to us.

The assurance of the biblical story is that God is present with us, and we are not alone, even when we are in pain. He is actively working to bring healing. I hope I can remember this when pain returns. Pain is somehow part of our humanity—a part we would rather not experience, but it's wired into who we are as people.

I wonder whether a parallel exists in nature about pain and new life. For women in childbirth, the pain of that most human of all experiences is mixed with indescribable joy as a new life enters the world and begins its earthly journey. Perhaps, in the same way, the pain we experience before death is followed by new life into a realm that we do not fully understand. In both birth and death, in our arrival and departure from this planet, pain brings new life. It is a pattern woven into the deepest fabric of creation itself.

I do not look forward to what will probably be intense pain again at some point in the future.

CHAPTER 11

WAITING

They that wait upon the Lord shall renew their strength.

Isaiah 40:31

When I await medical test results, I feel tightly strapped onto an emotional roller coaster. The waiting produces anxiety in my spirit. In times like this, I try to remind myself that God already knows the test results before I even go in for a blood draw.

A wise friend who prayed for me after a rise in my PSA in early summer 2022 encouraged me to "Look to the One who gives Life, not to the numbers."[19] I need to hear and remember this.

I do feel anxious while waiting for test results, what they may indicate, and whether I will be called home before finishing things important to me. This question, expressed by Jesus, is apt, even when I cannot put my anxieties to rest: "And which of you by being anxious can add one cubit to his span of life?" (Matthew 6:27).

Each time I have blood tests, scans, or other medical procedures—whether every few weeks or months or special tests, I feel I am taking a final exam over which I have no control. It reminds me of nightmares I have had over the years in which I find myself in school. I have forgotten to study for the final exam or even attend classes for most or all of the semester. Sometimes, I don't even know the location of the classroom! The wait for results produces this sense of desperation, hopelessness, and fear.

Though I try to promote healing and health, I realize I don't have full control over outcomes. I try to internalize the words of the psalmist who cries out to God that "My times are in thy hand." (Psalm 31:15). However, these words are small consolation as I try to allow my faith to conquer my fears. It's a continual struggle to allow my theology to drive my response.

One month after the dreadful diagnosis, I wrote in my journal about the first of many medical milestones and wondered whether my treatment would be effective.[20]

> It's very hard to live with the unknown of how many more days or months or years I have. Certainly, all of our days are limited but this is such a jolt that my time on this earth could end sooner than I anticipate. I won't know until early July, when I have another PSA test, whether the Lupron[21] is working. Sometimes I feel hip or back pains and think the treatment will not be helpful and I'll be dead before the end of the year. Other times, I think I'll be in the 5% unsuccessful category, and the doctor said in such a case I would have four to five more years. That makes me really sad. Other times I feel I'll beat this and live 20 or 25 more years. My life is in your hands, Lord.

Certainly, God numbers my days[22] and loves me. I can trust him with the life he has given to me. I know all of this in my head, but my worrying heart waits for when the other shoe will drop on my health. It's traumatic to live with such anxiety that triggers my dread of the unknown. Extended or drawn-out dread simply reinforces my anxiety. It's a vicious cycle.

I remind myself that dread is a normal human response to the unknown. It doesn't make it any easier to experience. Somehow, however,

God meets me in the here and now as I wait for results and for my days to play out. I know he is present and feels my pain.

As I wait for test results, I feel a sense of impending doom that doesn't go away even after I've received the test results. It is usually magnified. Each milestone brings me closer to the end of my earthly pilgrimage. Results often feel like a death sentence. I cry, get angry, and plunge into a spiraling depression. Mercifully, however, the sun always comes up the next morning, and after a few days I recover my emotional equilibrium. But that doesn't stop the vicious cycle from repeating itself. While I know that test results are just numbers or images, they do reflect the reality of what is going on inside my body. That scares me and fills me with fear and deep sadness.

Sometimes, more promising test results pleasantly surprise me, but I also realize the long-term trend line on my health isn't hopeful. Of course, new developments may offer a cure, but the cancer also eventually could strangle my life-force as it continues its relentless and aberrational growth.

Life feels so uncertain, even after test results come in. I don't know what the future will hold. I don't know the number of my days. I have to remind myself that I never knew how long I would live before I was diagnosed with cancer, just as I don't know that now. All I have is a bitter cocktail—the present moment with dread and joy mingled together.

EMOTIONAL JOURNEY

CHAPTER 12

SADNESS

Be happy in the moment; that's enough.
Each moment is all we need, not more.

Mother Teresa

While many emotions express what I have felt on this uncertain journey, sadness has been the most frequent and intensely felt. Many times, I am just incredibly, uncontrollably, and profoundly sad. I cry by myself and with others.

My biggest sadness comes from the thought of not being around for family and friends, leaving them in the lurch, and missing the joy of inter-action. I feel sad that I might not get to see my now 6-year-old grandson grow up. While I long to live to see him reach his adult years, I am all too aware that is highly unlikely.

The words of William Howard Taft, writing to his father about his chances of getting appointed to the Supreme Court by President Benjamin Harrison, are apt: "My chances of going to the moon and donning a silk gown at the hands of President Harrison are about equal."[23] I am sad because I will miss the love of family and experiencing life with so many dear and supportive friends.

My big concern, however, pertains to those I would leave behind. I don't want to hurt them. I don't want them to experience grief at my early passing. I feel guilty that I will impose on them since I will not be around to love and help them. I realize I have no control over the number of my days, but nevertheless, this is how I feel.

While I know that death is not the final word and that I will see loved ones in the life hereafter, the thought of losing deep, personal connections in the here and now makes me sad—for both me and them.

In one sense, I feel ready for God to call me home whenever he deems appropriate. My life has been full, and I have been successful and accomplished much.

In another sense, I definitely do not feel ready to leave. I am coming to a point of self-confidence. I feel I can really do some good in the world. Too much of my life still feels unfinished. I would miss the amazing people who have surrounded me and loved me. They have been God's good gift to me.

I'm sad I might not be able to do all the things I want to do in life. I might not live long enough to write all the things I want to write—to leave a legacy. I will miss the stunning beauty of God's creation and the marvels of human technology.

My sadness overwhelms and often paralyzes me. I also feel the pain of realizing that I will never escape the sadness of having prostate cancer. It will accompany me for the remainder of my days. How do I live with this sadness and not allow it to immobilize me? My challenge is how to hold my emotions in balance, particularly how to not let sadness overwhelm me so much that I forget that God walks with me each step of the way and holds my hand. He is the Lord of my journey.

Unexpected life events can traumatize us and sap our spirit. When Calvin Coolidge was president, his 16-year-old son, Calvin, Jr., developed a blister on his toe while playing tennis at the White House. The blister became infected and within a week he was dead from blood poisoning. Coolidge never recovered from this loss. He sank into a deep depression, and his natural persona as a man of few words only intensified. "I just can't believe it has happened," the president muttered through tears.[24] It felt surreal to him. This wasn't how things were supposed to be. Years later, in his autobiography, Coolidge wrote about his son's death, "When he went, the power and the glory of the Presidency went with him."[25]

I know that whether I live or die, I belong body, soul, and spirit to God, but that doesn't take away my sadness, and at times, depression.

So now, just as God has called me into life and breathed air into my lungs, and just as he has called me in life—in career, family, and friends—so now he is beginning to whisper to me about his next calling to me—when he calls me home to himself.

I will miss most the people who have been part of my life. I am also sad to be leaving them to walk their journeys without me. It's been such an honor and gift to walk alongside so many people. God has given me a high dose of creativity and ideas, and I will miss not being able to implement my dreams. We pass from this life into the next just once, and none of us knows what it will be like. If I trust that God is good and loving, however, it will be a good new existence. But for now, being bound by time and space is all I know.

My heart is often profoundly sad and downcast. I teeter on the edge of depression. I long for sustaining hope in the winter of my heart.

CHAPTER 13

UNFAIRNESS

He has broken my strength in mid-course;
he has shortened my days.
"O my God," I say,
"take me not hence in the midst of my days,
thou whose years endure throughout all generations!

Psalm 102:23-24

As I initially responded to this unexpected and surreal diagnosis, God seemed remote, and I was angry with him. How could he allow this to happen to me? I have tried hard to live well, although I know I am not perfect. Is there no reward for faithfulness?

More than that, I struggle with the deep and pervasive feeling that getting cancer just isn't fair. Why me? Why now? It seems so random. This feeling of unfairness stems from my expectation that I will live a long life and enjoy good health, despite having less than robust family genes and dismal family longevity. I have done the right things to take care of this body God has gifted me with for the journey. Doing so, I thought, should delay my eventual death. Maybe my actions have helped and are helping. I don't know. Nevertheless, it all feels unfair.

I guess I have not gotten over the shock of my sudden decline with the cancer and the seeming unfairness of having a life-threatening illness at too young an age.

Yet I need to remember that death is a part of life. I hadn't thought much about it or planned for it, perhaps because I had gone for so long without health issues. Somehow, I thought I would escape disease, or at least not have it come upon me in my 60s.

According to the U.S. Census Bureau, I already have lived a long life. People over 65 constitute just 16.5% of the population, meaning my days are statistically narrowing.[26] Still, I never have thought of myself as old. A good friend reminded me that I am an old man. That was a shock to my system as I have always felt young. In one sense, recognizing that I am older from the perspective of statistics and life expectancy is encouraging. It makes the cancer feel less unfair and helps me to view it in the grand arc of human history. It helps me to adjust my youthful and rose-colored expectations.

I have thought about how I would respond to the same diagnosis if I were 85 and not 65. Clearly, I wouldn't be happy, and would want to live longer, assuming I was in otherwise good health. I would, however, feel better having lived a longer life. Perhaps, by God's grace, I might yet live to 85. My expiration date remains a mystery.

I often read the obituaries in the Sunday newspaper. They tell the stories of people who have lived amazing and full lives of accomplishment and relationships. The obituaries help normalize my situation and reinforce the reality that, regardless of the age we pass away, we will all die. The passing of others somehow makes me feel less alone and reduces my sense of unfairness at what I view as the untimely failing of my body.

Obituaries are sobering reminders that my days in this time-and-space-bound existence are narrowing, and my time is coming when life will end for me. Reading these summaries of the lives of others also inspires me to view each moment as precious and to live well in the days I have remaining, and to make a difference in this world.

But my overall feeling—and simmering depression—that this is unfair seems to be grounded in the fact that I am in still in my 60s and have taken care of myself. I have watched what I have eaten. I have maintained a healthy weight. I haven't smoked, drunk alcohol, or done drugs. I have exercised. I am befuddled that I should get cancer when I am so healthy otherwise.

Once (okay, maybe it was more than once), I complained to a friend that the onset of cancerous cells in my body at an early age was unfair. She wisely responded with the following:

> Yes, I understand the "unfair" mindset, but it's all part of the plan. It's just a way to get you to your transformation day. We will all get there. Just the path is unknown. It's only "unfair" in a human mindset, not through an eternal perspective.[27]

In the long history of the world, I understand that people die at different ages—sometimes young. There are no guarantees. I have known people who have abused their bodies and lived into their 90s, and people who have respected and cared for their bodies who have died younger than I was when I was diagnosed with cancer at 65.

It's a lonely journey for me to think I am blazing a trail with a potential early demise, or at least an early diagnosis, when I have friends and acquaintances who are my age and older who are still living, going strong, and will be left behind when I pass away. I don't want to be a trailblazer on this. I don't want to leave this earth so soon before others who are close to me.

In spring 2022, I talked with a good and long-term friend my age who was musing about the fact he probably has perhaps 20 or so more years. Jeff's recognition of his mortality, in a strange way, made me feel better and less lonely, that I am not the only one facing my mortality. I am facing it more immediately and intensely than he is, but in the grand scheme of things, the ravages of time will hit all of us.

In the early months of the COVID-19 pandemic, I had a phone call with a dear and wise friend of almost a half-century. I told Jo Dee that my diagnosis felt unfair. She challenged me to dig more deeply into what was behind that thought.

Certainly, I would be less than human if I didn't experience deep internal conflicts. I wanted, however, to understand more fully what was behind my feelings of unfairness.

In one sense, my feelings are grounded in unmet expectations, which is probably always the case when we feel something is unfair. We don't expect bad things to happen to us. Should I really have an expectation that my health will always be good? I have expected it to be good since it's always been good. I chalked up multiple aches as just part of aging and not part of more systemic and serious problems.

Should I expect to live long? My family genes are not impressive, with a host of heart attacks and strokes and a variety of cancers coming on at early ages. By family genetics, I am an old man, and I am living on borrowed time.

I think my feelings of unfairness arise because of shock. I feel I am in the prime of my life—full of energy, calling, vision, hopes, and dreams. I don't FEEL like an old man and never have. Should I have expected the cancer? No. Should I have expected something to hit me at some point? Sure.

If I remember that all of life and every day is a gift, I also should expect that I have no right to this gift of life. I am not my own. I have been "bought with a price." (1 Corinthians 6:20). And because life is a gift, I have no rights. I live by grace alone.

This is where it gets tricky. Certainly, part of me says that if I have taken care of this body (not perfectly of course but better than most), God somehow owes me good health and long life. But that doesn't work with a gift. Even so, how I treat my body correlates with my health. In other words, I cannot abuse the gift of the body without negative consequences. But simply taking care of it doesn't guarantee good health.

This is where I have to hold lightly this balance between the gift and my actions. This tension shows up in so many other areas.

To cry "unfair" is to say I have been wronged by the giver of life. It is to demand (or at least strongly expect) that I be immune from the ravages of time, genetics, and chance. It is to fail to acknowledge God's grace.

It's easier for me to say it's okay to get cancer and die when I am in my 80s than in my late 60s. I am grateful for this life at my age now and hope I would be similarly grateful if disease waited until I was older. I was blessed with 65 years of great health, which not everyone has experienced.

I need to get over my sense of unfairness. I think I am making progress on that. I am still dealing with the shock of my disintegrating body. As my new reality sinks in each day, I continue to take steps to strengthen my body. Perhaps this aging body can heal itself through the amazingly complex systems God has created. More likely, I am realizing, based on the nature of metastatic prostate cancer, my days are more limited than I would like.

To say it's "unfair" ignores God's grace and what I should be expecting, which is death, save for the work of Jesus. Yes, I will die one day. This body ultimately will fail. But "I" am more than this body which is but a temporary house for my soul and spirit. And the death that "I" deserve has been wiped away by the death of Jesus and by God's grace. Certainly, this body will turn back into the dust of the earth.

Instead of demanding my "rights" to good health, I need to remember life is pure grace. The wisdom of author and theologian Frederick Buechner particularly applies:

Listen to your life. See it for the fathomless mystery that it is. In the boredom and pain of it no less than in the excitement and gladness: touch, taste, smell your way to the holy and hidden heart of it because in the last analysis all moments are key moments and life itself is grace.[28]

If I can reframe my heart along these lines, my heart will turn more to thanksgiving rather than complaining about how unfair it is. Gratitude is an antidote to unfairness. I am genuinely grateful for so many things in life. In so many ways, God has blessed me with a wonderful life.

More and more, I am grateful to wake up each morning to a new day. Prior to the cancer diagnosis, I never was seriously ill a day in my life. I have enjoyed amazing health. I am grateful for the caring and skilled medical professionals I have been privileged to meet.

I am grateful for family and friends—for being surrounded by so many who have encouraged me, prayed with and for me, and walked this difficult journey with me.

I am grateful for the many and varied careers God has called me to—from university administrator to government contracting manager, to self-employed consultant, and now to presidential historian.

I have had a great career in management and public contracting that enabled me to provide financially for my family and launch my children into the world with plenty of experiences and resources. I have been recognized nationally and locally by the public procurement profession. I have had an amazing run at being a consultant that has been fulfilling, enabled me to help others, and be appreciated. My consulting and training have given me the chances to travel, including to many presidential sites

I have reinvented myself as a presidential historian. That has been one of the biggest and most pleasant surprises of my life. I never imagined I could hang up my historian shingle and get recognized by the media. I have written and published two books about the presidents.[29] It's been such a joy to indulge in this lifelong interest in the presidents.

I have been blessed with wonderful friends whose companionship I continue to enjoy. They have surrounded me with prayers, encouragement, love, and support. I find that I am more of an extrovert than I ever thought I was. I have grown more self-confident.

Regardless of my gratitude, this is just a hard journey, and thoughts of how this is so unfair continue to plague my thinking.

For most of this journey since I was diagnosed, I have felt good physically. I have assembled a wonderful medical team. My side effects from the treatments are manageable most of the time, especially when I know how much so many other men are suffering with far greater impacts. I am aware, though, this will likely change for me at some point.

My challenge is to accept and embrace my new reality. I need to rise to the occasion (which I think I am doing most of the time) rather than complain about how unfair it is. Unfairness is a natural reaction at the time of a diagnosis. It's an initial emotional response. But as I reflect on it with gentle prodding from my friend, I see that I need to move beyond that—from unfairness to gratitude.

What a journey this is! There is so much for which I am thankful. It's just sad that it may be coming to an end soon.

I don't know the stops along the way of this journey. All I know is that I will be girded every step by my gracious Father and that he is walking with me. I want my heart to be shaped by his heart and to long for him, regardless of the to-be-expected unexpected and unknown stops along the way that undoubtedly will involve pain.

Whether my journey is a short one or a long one, I belong in body, soul, and spirit to my loving Father and Creator, and each day of the journey is a gift, not a right. I am the creature, not the creator and my life is not my own. I try to remind myself that God numbers my days and that I won't die before the day appointed for me by his sovereign will. But that doesn't make this journey less sad, and it doesn't really deal with my anger, frustration, fear, and the sense that getting cancer at this age just is not fair.

I will continue to work diligently in partnership with my sovereign God for my healing and to trust him for the life he's given to me. Maybe this is part of what it means for me to live well with uncertainty.

This isn't how I expected to be spending my retirement years. It feels unfair that I struggle just to stay alive while others who haven't taken care of their bodies can live without concern that their days are coming to an end. Maybe I am the one who is blessed since I know my days will end. Even should I live to 75 or older, at least I have a deeper appreciation of each moment and each encounter, knowing that the rapidly multiplying cells in my body eventually will snuff the life out of me. I can live deliberately now. It's a small consolation.

As someone who understands history, I know that people come and go and that we make a difference here for such a short time. But still, I have so much more I want to do, and I am not ready. It's about impact and legacy.

It's been a slow realization for me emotionally to internalize that it is God who determines the number of my days and not me. While I have always understood that intellectually and theologically, this slow deterioration of my body, despite the fact that I want to control my health and extend my days, isn't something over which I have control. I am slowly growing into a more comfortable place where I am more accepting of the reality that my Creator may choose, for whatever reasons, to limit my days and not allow me to live a long life here. So, I resolve that I want to live well, fully and faithfully, in whatever days I am given on this earth.

The following prayer, "When Dying Feels Unfair" (used by permission) resonates deeply with my heart and I tear up every time I read it.[30]

O Christ Most Merciful,

O Christ Ever Just,

Here I am again, feeling there must be some mistake to the numbering of my days, in the ways my remaining hours so rapidly dwindle toward an unwanted end whose approach I cannot slow.

I am like a child, O Lord, who knows the injustice of an early bedtime imposed while the house is full of feasting and songs and stories and laughter.

I do not want to leave this life. I do not want to leave this place and time.

I do not want to fold and tuck away the remains of my days, while the rest of the world—like water roiling around a river rock—rushes past me, moving faster than I can follow.

Will they simply carry on without me—these stories, these people, this ceaseless unspooling of moments spinning past into memory?

I do not want to leave this life, O Lord. I do not want to be unwoven from the world. My heart cries out:

Unfair! Unfair!

Can you not call a halt to my dying till some time hence when my race might finally feel complete, and not as if I had suddenly stumbled, my muscles giving out in the midst of a marathon my heart yearns yet to run?

I do not want to simply reach the end, Jesus. I want to finish, and I want to finish well.

This is not my will.

I do not want to die so soon, so inconveniently, half feeling the need to apologize for my own mortality, as if by dying I had somehow failed— like inspiration fizzling out in a poet's mind before the rhyme is found.

This is not my will.

This is not my chosen way or time. Is it yours? It is not mine. But is it yours?

How could it be?

CHAPTER 14

GRIEF

Grief is the price we pay for love.

Queen Elizabeth II

I am all too acquainted with intense grief in this season of life. It has been my constant companion. I grieve the death of my dreams about the future, my disintegrating health with corresponding limitations of what I can do physically, the anguish of leaving loved ones behind, the heartache of not experiencing the beauty and wonder of this world.

The subjects of my grief all deal with loss or potential loss. I know loss is a part of life, but I hope that I somehow will be shielded from it—that I will live in a fantasy world in which bad things don't happen. What makes grief hard is that it rears its ugly head when we least expect it. It catches us by surprise and throws us off balance. We experience disappointment and grief when our expectations are shattered.

I didn't expect I would be diagnosed with an incurable and life-threatening cancer when I was 65 and in otherwise excellent health. I didn't expect my plans for the future to become vanishing dreams. I didn't expect that I might need to say goodbye to family and dear friends so soon. I expected I would live at least well into my 70s given my otherwise excellent health. While that might yet occur, it doesn't seem likely. It's hard to fathom not being able to experience the joys and beauty of this world.

One hot morning when I was in Merced, Calif. on a walk, before continuing my marathon drive from Seattle to Southern California for my 50th high-school reunion, I stopped to look at a small and non-descript building. It was formerly a drive-through coffee stand, but it had long since boarded its doors and shuttered its windows. Whoever owned it once had dreams of a thriving business. Something happened, though. Maybe there wasn't enough business, or the owner had health issues. Regardless, once bright and promising dreams were shuttered like the plywood-covered windows, leaving the building to decay and weeds to grow. Certainly, the owner experienced grief at the death of his or her dreams. Customers likewise grieved the loss. Grief is an unfortunate part of life.

So, how do I deal with my grief? My expectations are real and my dreams promising, but they are being dashed before my eyes. How do I live well in the midst of grief? I need to acknowledge the reality of my grief and that things don't always go according to my plans.

Perhaps my first task is to process, understand, and live with the pain. I would rather skip this step. I don't like living with the discomfort of my raw emotions. I like being in control, living objectively in my head and not having my heart wrenched.

I grieve when expectations vanish before my eyes. Acknowledging and processing my pain is an important and difficult part of moving forward and living well today.

After I have grown in processing and acknowledging the reality of my emotional pain, perhaps I can move forward in accepting the reality of my failing health. This is hard for me. It feels surreal to think I am dying. How is this happening when I have been healthy my whole life and I am still relatively young? Surely, this cannot be happening to me. It must be just a vivid, tragic nightmare.

Unfortunately, this is a living nightmare. It's real. This body God gave to me for this earthly journey is turning on itself. As much as I would like to do so, I can't put my head in the sand and ignore what is happening. I need to face reality and gradually, and hopefully gracefully, move to a place of acceptance. I want to employ all the resources I can muster to take care of my body in however many days remain for me and continue to do the work to which I feel called.

Beyond processing my grief and accepting unfulfilled expectations, I have slowly adjusted to this new reality. Researching health issues and going to medical appointments was never what I wanted to do. But it is what I do now. I could spend my emotional energy suppressing reality, but to what purpose? Experiencing grief is an important part of life though something I would prefer to ignore.

Despite my grief from unfulfilled expectations, I try to live in the present. I can't change the past or control the future. All I can do is to live well in the moment, to engage fully with life, while still acknowledging the pain I feel.

In my grief and fear, I need to remember to listen for God's voice and sense his presence. Though he often feels distant, he walks with me, holding my hand each step of this uncertain journey.

After I left my 50th high school reunion, despite the joy of encounters with classmates, I grieved the loss of future friendships. The conversations accentuated my fragile health and not knowing what the future has in store for me. I grieved as I realized the reunion was the last time I would see most, if not all, of these friends. I also grieved about what these friends would face in the remaining years of their lives and what heartache and health challenges they would experience.

CHAPTER 15

DESPAIR

When I tread the verge of Jordan,
bid my anxious fears subside.

Guide Me, Oh Thou Great Jehovah hymn

One challenge of living with cancer is that it introduces everyday uncertainty. I don't know when the cancer will shut my body down. Maybe everything I have done to promote my health will keep the cancer at bay for many more years. Maybe a cure for metastatic prostate cancer will emerge while I can benefit from it. Maybe the cancer will follow a statistical average and I will die from it far sooner than I thought my life would end. I simply don't know.

In one sense, I can frame my health-promoting practices and cancer-reducing treatments as an interlude—to beat the statistical odds and be cured, or to death. Regardless, all any of us is given is the present moment. My present moments are but an interlude to a mysteriously shrouded future that unfolds and emerges slowly and uncertainly.

Each day, therefore is, as one dear friend reminds me, a hike up what we have dubbed Mount Interlude. Sometimes the path is level, and I can walk easily, not out of breath, and enjoy the scenery. Other times, the path begins a sharp ascent, and it takes all my focus to stay on the path and not stumble while my breathing becomes labored. In times like this, it's harder for me to soak in the beauty of trees and breathe the forest air. At times, boulders, rocks, and huge tree roots block my path. Sometimes, I'm out of breath and need to take a break. Other times, I need to stop at a first-aid station to bandage scrapes from a trip and fall. When cool clouds enshroud the trail, I see only a few feet before me, and I walk slowly and cautiously. My goal is to press forward, trying to enjoy the scenery of the moment while sometimes struggling with the exertion required on parts of the hike.

So, I trek up Mount Interlude, not knowing how long the hike will last or what I will encounter. I don't know when I will reach the top or what views and experiences await me. I know only that in the immediacy of each moment I will experience deep beauty and terrifying unpredictability.

I don't know whether reaching the pinnacle of Mount Interlude will represent healing, about which I once was more optimistic, or reaching the end of my years here. I wonder what my transformed life in a new world will be like.

On this hike, my emotions vacillate from hope to realism to despair. Sometimes I hope that I beat the odds and that my body is strong enough to suppress the cancerous cells into submission as they rejoin the community of healthy cells. If not that, I hope that I significantly beat the averages for the length of effective treatments, especially given that I probably am doing a lot more than many men in a similar situation and am in otherwise excellent health.

At one point, a friend provided encouragement. She said that because I am doing so much to promote my health that once the cancer is gone, I will be ready for another 30 or so years. That is certainly my hope as well.

Sometimes, I feel my hope is artificial and not grounded in reality. On what is my hope built? I could ignore the reality of the seriousness of this particular form of cancer and simply listen to voices that tell me I will beat the cancer. While they mean well by encouraging me, those who say that to me often do not know that metastatic prostate cancer has no cure and that I live with a chronic and terminal condition. Thus, my realism begins to creep in and to drown out voices of hope.

My hope also melts into the realism of statistical survival rates. My response, then, is to pack in as much life as I can before I become yet another statistic.

I can't remain in the realism mode for long without plunging into deep despair and sadness. At these times, I melt down, and my tears flow uncontrollably.

The balance among hope, realism, and despair is fluid and constantly changing. It's hard to remain balanced and keep these emotions from whiplashing me.

In a classic scene from "Fiddler on the Roof," the fiddler makes music while balanced precariously on the slope of the roof. His feet hold firm against distraction and "an unexpected breeze [that] could blow him to the ground."[31] I feel like I'm the fiddler, trying to keep my balance between hope and realism without losing my footing and plunging into despair.

A similar image that comes to mind has me standing atop of a high, plateaued rock formation. A long linear crack splits the rock into two sections—a rock of hope and a rock of realism. With my legs spread over the split, I need to keep my balance and not plunge into the deep chasm of despair.

I lose my balance when my emotions overcome me. When I feel cancer-related discomfort or pain I begin to catastrophize with a sense of impending doom. The brutal realism of the medical world is also depressing.

Faith stands in the gap between hope and the uncertainty caused by realism and despair. Ideally, my faith in God sustains me and keeps me from losing my balance. The knowledge that God has lovingly created both me and the universe and brings new life should and sometimes does sustain me. When it does, I remain focused on hope and living fully in the here and now. My emotions, however, do overtake me at times, and I lose focus. I fall into the abyss or lose my balance fiddling on the roof.

While I want to live more in hope rather than despair, despite my head knowledge, I know my emotions will overtake me at times and I will lose my balance and fall. I stumble on my hike up Mount Interlude. To deal with this, my strategy has been to be mindful, live in the moment, and focus on gratitude. Concentrating on a task at hand, breathing deeply, being in nature, and listening to music all have helped arrest my descent into emotional instability. Sometimes it works, and sometimes it doesn't.

May God give me the eyes to see him clearly in the ordinary and extraordinary moments of today.

CHAPTER 16

TEARS

Weeping may endure for a night,
but joy cometh in the morning.

Psalm 30:5 (King James Version)

On this uncertain journey, I have shed many tears.

Sometimes they are triggered by physical fatigue induced by radiation or chemotherapy. Sometimes, they flow when exhaustion emerges toward the end of a day. My body is less resilient while using internal resources to promote healing. Fatigue impairs my equilibrium and stirs my emotions. In times like this, nothing seems good or right. I viscerally understand why toddlers cry when they are tired.

I also have melted down when receiving less than positive blood-test or scan results.

Sometimes I cry not because of fatigue or bad news, but because people have loved me in deep ways and more than I feel I deserve. Those are tears of joy.

Many times, when I talk with family or friends, I begin to share something about my situation, and I feel tears unexpectedly welling up inside me. I pause, hoping my off-guard emotional intensity will pass. I continue speaking but can't ignore the grief. I break down crying. It is part of my humanity.

In a live Facebook event in spring 2022, a friend sang and prayed to encourage those listening. At one point, she directed her words and music to me specifically while singing the praise song "He Touched Me." When she mentioned my name and sang, I couldn't contain myself. I deeply experienced the moment. My tears of sadness, comfort, and joy blended as her gesture deeply touched my heart.[32]

I remind myself it is to be expected I will cry as I face an unknown future, as my sadness over the death of my expectations overtakes my spirit, and as the reality of my failing health settles over my soul like a heavy fog.

Testosterone-blocking medications certainly contribute to my emotional fragility and hair-trigger tears. With my testosterone levels low to starve the cancer, I am less able to control my emotions.

Tears are often an expression that things in this world aren't right. Tears are part of what it means to be human. It's okay to cry. That's good because I do it a lot. Even Jesus wept when he was told of the death of his good friend Lazarus.[33]

In May 2021, I was asked by the pastor at my church to lead a worship service. For 20 years I have done this often and always have enjoyed it, even though it takes a lot of preparation. This time, I was surprised at my response. I felt overwhelming weariness. I felt like crying. I felt spiritually bankrupt. I didn't want to make or take time to prepare. I didn't have the energy, nor did I feel like I had anything to contribute. On the other hand, I felt a sense of obligation to share my gifts and perspectives with the congregation.

I met with Alyssa, my counselor, sharing my tension between feeling weariness and guilt. I was torn. She advised me to take care of myself by setting boundaries. She reminded me that someone else could lead worship.

What surprised me most, however, was how I responded when I shared this dilemma with her. I teared up, reflecting that my emotions were far more raw and closer to the surface than I thought. I was emotionally fragile.

I know tears will continue to be part of this journey. However, I don't want to become so immobilized that I fail to fully engage in life. Words from the Apostle Paul's second letter to the church at Corinth resonate with me: "So we do not lose heart. Though our outer nature is wasting away, our inner nature is being renewed every day." (2 Corinthians 4:16).

CHAPTER 17

FUTURE-TRIPPING

God does not bid us bear the burdens of tomorrow, next week, or next year. Every day we are to come to Him in simple obedience and faith, asking help to keep us, and aid us through that day's work; and tomorrow, and tomorrow, and tomorrow, through years of long tomorrows, it will be but the same thing to do; leaving the future always in God's hands, sure that He can care for it better than we. Blessed trust! that can thus confidingly say, "This hour is mine with its present duty; the next is God's, and when it comes, God's presence will come with it.
William Reed Huntington, 19th Century Episcopal priest

I confess that I am an expert at the fine-art form called future-tripping, also known as anticipatory anxiety.

I easily catastrophize pain by worrying that my end is drawing closer. Certainly, it may be true at any moment, but I may need to endure and learn from pain as part of being human. Can I turn my pain into a place of grace from God and others? How can I control the future-tripping to focus on the present moment?

Unfortunate news can produce a spectrum of responses. At one end, I can future-trip. At the other end, I can remain hopeful. I need to settle somewhere in the middle on realism.

Alyssa, my counselor, advised me to create a self-care plan to put boundaries around less-than-positive medical-test results. She reassured me that it is normal to grieve a higher PSA or a scan that shows continued cancer growth. But wallowing in grief doesn't help matters because it distracts me from doing things to which I feel called. Alyssa suggested I put a limit of 30 minutes on grieving. Then I should call friends with whom I can process the results. Going for a walk, especially in a forested area can help me keep things in perspective. I also have allowed myself to indulge in pizza or ice-cream.

Another feature of a self-care plan is to write believable, positive affirmations that can ground me. Here are some examples:

- I make good decisions even if they don't lead to desired outcomes.
- I make the best decisions I can at the time.

The antidote to future-tripping is to focus on living in the moment, which is really all any of us are given. How do I distract my racing mind from drawing catastrophic conclusions based on test results over which I have no control?

Slowly, I am accepting that cancer may result in a shorter life than I ever imagined. In the long history of the world, individuals exist on this planet for only a relatively short time. I am part of that grand history. Whether I live to my late 60s or longer, I aim to live well in the moments and days I have been given. I try to remember that.

Staying busy and focused on good work keeps me from future-tripping. One of the best examples is writing. As I write, I tune out the world and forget my fears.

Living in the moment distracts my thoughts as they come, allows me to listen to and pay attention to myself breathing deeply, and keeps me still. In what is called mindfulness, I can pay attention to the sights and smells as I walk, curiously noticing the details of trees, birds, cats, and dogs. On one walk, I marveled at the graceful beauty of a horse grazing in a field. I stopped to smell flowers and took pictures of particularly beautiful blossoms.

I can stay in the moment by:

- Focusing on the taste of foods.

- Watching online videos of peaceful rivers flowing over rocks, complete with the magical water sounds.

- Listening to music, allowing myself to be drawn into the splendor of the words and notes. Singing hymns and praise songs with good words instructs my mind theologically when I can't focus and fills me with hope. My spirit soars. In addition, Mozart draws my spirit into the moment.

My goal in these activities is to let my mind be in the here and now. Sometimes my mind wanders to the future, and I worry. I try to keep pulling myself back to the present.

Another way to think about mindfulness to reduce the soul trauma of future-tripping is to think about tomorrow in ways that have boundaries and guardrails that bring my thinking back to today.

None of this is easy. It's natural for me to grieve a bad test result or worry because of a new pain. It's okay for me to experience these things as long as I don't let them to consume me. Alyssa, my counselor, thinks that I am succeeding in living in the present and embracing relationships, and that I am living faithfully. That's encouraging because I don't always feel that. After one rise in my PSA in March 2021, Alyssa described my response as both hopelessness and determination, which I think is fairly accurate. It was nice to get that affirmation. Sometimes, I'm more successful than others in living in the moment.

On May 20, 2022, I received an updated PSA result, along with my white and red blood counts. The results were not promising. My PSA rose from 14.6 to 16.2 despite my having been on chemotherapy for seven months. My white blood counts tanked, putting into question whether my body was strong enough for another round of chemo.

I began my future-tripping. The negative results sent me into a tailspin of discouragement and sadness. I have done all the right things about my health, yet nothing seemed to make a difference. My treatments haven't reduced the PSA, reflecting the growth of the cancer.

Would I be healthy enough to go on a two-week retreat to work on this book? (Yes, I was.) Could I finish this book? (You're reading it now.) Similarly, could I finish writing a book about government construction contracting that I was asked to write? (I finished it.) Could I attend my 50th high school reunion in July? (I went and had a wonderful time.)

It was easy for me to get wrapped up with the immediacy of negative test results and forget how to practice mindfulness. Maybe I'll remember the next time. I know I will have plenty of new opportunities to practice these techniques to manage stress and reduce my tendency of future-tripping.

CHAPTER 18

COUNSELING

This is my wish for you: Comfort on difficult days, smiles when sadness intrudes, rainbows to follow the clouds, laughter to kiss your lips, sunsets to warm your heart, hugs when spirits sag, beauty for your eyes to see, friendships to brighten your being, faith so that you can believe, confidence for when you doubt, courage to know yourself, patience to accept the truth, Love to complete your life.

Ralph Waldo Emerson

Fall 2019 was a difficult season. I had been diagnosed with stage 4 prostate cancer in May. I had just learned from my urologist the depressing news that my statistical chance of surviving the cancer for five years was only 30%. It also was when I switched my care from a urologist to an oncologist. I began additional treatments to suppress the production of testosterone and strengthen my bones that were being eaten away by growing cancer cells. My medications caused hot flashes and other side effects. I decided it was important to pay attention to how I was coping emotionally on this roller coaster ride.

I needed a counselor but the thought of finding one was too much for me to handle. My wife, Catherine, generously researched counselors and gave me a list of four to consider. That was helpful. I contacted a counselor who seemed like the best fit for me, and Cathy agreed to begin meeting with me. In the first session she asked standard questions about my background. While this was an emotionally difficult time, I felt I had a fairly good sense of the situation.

After the second session, during which Cathy had simply listened to me without asking questions or provided any advice or perspective based on her years of experience as a counselor, I told her that for the counseling to be effective, I needed her to be more interactive. Unfortunately, she never changed her approach. The sessions became gripe sessions with me bemoaning the same issues on which I felt stuck and with her simply listening. Usually at the end of each session, she would offer up one routine catchphrase of advice, but that seemed shallow.

As I approached meeting with her after a half-dozen sessions, it became clear that this was not a useful exercise. I began dreading the sessions. They made me feel more hopeless, and her lack of input didn't help me cope with the cancer and other issues with which I was dealing. I felt like all I was doing was whining. I have many wonderful friends who listen to me, but I needed someone who could provide tangible advice and tools to help me deal with my situation. I emailed her in February 2020 canceling our upcoming appointment and future sessions.

No doubt Cathy is a wonderful counselor for some people. It simply wasn't a good match for me and my needs at that time. I was discouraged, though, and felt like no available resources could help me process the craziness of my life. Unfortunately, the experience reinforced my stereotypically negative image of counseling, including that nothing in a counseling relationship could help me.

Over the next year, I thought periodically about my continued need for a wise counselor to walk with me on this journey. I still felt I needed something more than what family and friends could offer. I decided to take the plunge again after a disappointing initial start of counseling.

In summer 2020, I searched online for a Christian counselor. Having a counselor who shared my world view and faith perspective was important for me. However, I didn't want a counselor who would be overly simplistic and piously religious in dealing with very tough issues. Online, I read dozens of profiles of counselors. Only one stood out as a potential match. I was struck by her characterization of her approach—that she could provide unconditional, positive regard and empathy, that she would be honored to walk the journey, and that she offered a warm, comfortable setting filled with conversations that deepen self-awareness. Those catchphrases resonated with me, but I didn't follow-up for another six months.

As 2021 dawned, I tried to remain positive, but found myself immersed in dark thoughts of the dismal realism of my situation. I often sunk into despair. I wasn't depressed and was living a full life with more things to do than I had time for, but I was experiencing hair-trigger tears.

I mentioned my emerging thinking to my acupuncturist that perhaps I needed to find a counselor. She agreed it might be a good strategy for me.

So, I conducted the same online search and came up with the same result. I finally contacted Alyssa even though her website stated she was taking no new clients. She told me her website was outdated, and she was willing to meet with me.

After two sessions with Alyssa, I told her it would be helpful for her to ask questions, provide input, and not simply listen to me. She took the cue and became much more interactive.

She has been effective in spite of the COVID-19 era. I met a few times with her in person, either outside or in her office with masks, but with my compromised immune system, most of my sessions with Alyssa have been conducted virtually. She has proven to be wise, biblical, an incredibly valuable resource, and a compassionate partner for the journey. She hasn't solved all my problems, but she has given me tools, strategies, attitudes, and approaches. More than anything, she has affirmed me, validated my feelings and my situation, and empathized deeply with what I face.

SPIRITUAL JOURNEY

CHAPTER 19

EQUILIBRIUM

*Life with God has its ups and its downs—those mountain
top highs of knowing and sensing his presence and guidance
in our lives, as well as the dark experiences in the valley
where God seems to be on an extended vacation.*[34]

Mike Purdy

A DISTANT GOD

Being diagnosed with metastatic prostate cancer has disrupted my spiritual equilibrium. Praying and studying the Bible have challenged me more as pain and worry have impeded my spiritual life. God often has seemed silent as I have struggled to maintain a semblance of normality in the face of my deteriorating health. I feel that God has abandoned me on this lonely journey.

For most of my adult life, ever since I embraced the truth of the Christian faith as a college freshman, I have been fairly disciplined in reading the Bible and praying daily. However, since the diagnosis, I have become distracted as I have focused on and worried about my health. I haven't possessed enough emotional or spiritual energy to maintain such disciplines. I have felt numb. I haven't had the stamina to be spiritual. Besides, part of me feels disappointed that my faithfulness over the years has not been rewarded with good health. Even so, I realize there are no guarantees in life and that God "sends rain on the just and on the unjust." (Matthew 5:45).

Certainly, I have prayed, but I have found it harder at times. God has seemed distant. My prayers have sometimes felt like prayers of desperation as I've cried out to God to heal me. This, I tell myself, can't be happening to me. "Oh, Lord, hear my prayer."

In these times, I remind myself that God is not a celestial vending machine who grants our every wish as we pray. Certainly, he could, but for reasons I do not understand, he mostly allows events to take their course and doesn't intervene by providing miracles.

Miraculously, he could heal me. But regardless of what happens to me, I remember he is the Lord and Creator of all life, and he is truth and love regardless of what I may experience. I don't love him because he does exactly what I ask, but because he loves me and has created me in love. As desperate as my prayers have felt, prayer is also a form of hope that God may yet intercede. As my PSA has risen and my pain has refused to vanish, I feel as if my petitions to God have fallen on deaf ears.

"DEVOTIONAL LITE"

Alyssa, my counselor, helpfully advised me how to maintain spiritual vitality in the midst of what seem like desert times. She encouraged me to relax and not feel as though my quiet times with God need to be as intellectual or robust as they once were. I could be more passive and experiential. "Devotional Lite," I call it.

I could read a small section of the Bible to experience it instead of mastering it intellectually. I could handwrite the words of scripture to help focus my mind on the message (something I have done previously to help memorize verses). I could read from an inspirational book in small chunks (a good friend has sent me devotional guides that I have read occasionally).

I have had limited success in following Alyssa's "devotional lite" advice because I have been too busy trying to pack in as much as I can into each day. Dealing with my emotions and not feeling well physically also have limited me.

At one point, I posted Psalm 145 on the bathroom wall and memorized it. This helped me remember God's power and work and kept my mind focused on truth rather than future-tripping.

> I will extol thee, my God and King, and bless thy name for ever and ever. Every day I will bless thee and praise thy name for ever and ever. Great is the LORD, and greatly to be praised, and his greatness is unsearchable. One generation shall laud thy works to another and shall declare thy mighty acts. On the glorious splendor of thy majesty, and on thy wondrous works, I will meditate. Men shall proclaim the might of thy terrible acts, and I will declare thy greatness. They shall pour forth the fame of thy abundant goodness and shall sing aloud of thy righteousness. The LORD is gracious and merciful, slow to anger and abounding in steadfast love. The LORD is good to all, and his compassion is over all that he has made. All thy works shall give thanks to thee, O LORD, and all thy saints shall bless thee! They shall speak of the glory of thy kingdom, and tell of thy power, to make known to the sons of men thy mighty deeds, and the glorious splendor of thy kingdom. Thy kingdom is an everlasting kingdom, and thy dominion endures throughout all generations. The LORD is faithful in all his words, and gracious in all his deeds. The LORD upholds all who are falling and raises up all who are bowed down. The eyes of all look to thee, and thou givest them their food in due season. Thou openest thy hand, thou satisfiest the desire of every living thing. The LORD is just in all his ways, and kind in all his doings. The LORD is near to all who call upon him, to all who call upon him in truth. He fulfils the desire of all who fear him, he also hears their cry, and saves

them. The LORD preserves all who love him; but all the wicked he will destroy. My mouth will speak the praise of the LORD, and let all flesh bless his holy name for ever and ever.

Despite struggling to maintain my spiritual equilibrium, none of it has changed my confidence that my creator God is ultimately sovereign over all of life, and he holds my life in his hands.

MUSIC FILLS MY SOUL

Music of hymns and spiritual praise songs, especially those I have memorized, have instructed to my mind and soothed my heart. When my mind and spirit can't find comfort in reading and being encouraged by scripture, singing hymns has brough me rich content. The lyrics teach me and encourage my heart, and the music inspires and calms my troubled soul.

Sometimes, I sing hymns on my morning walk. Meaningful phrases include:

- Tune my heart to sing thy grace.[35]
- Streams of mercy never ceasing.[36]
- Echoes of mercy, whispers of love.[37]
- Filled with his goodness, lost in His love.[38]
- The triumphs of his grace.[39]
- The glories of my God and King.[40]
- Disperse the gloomy clouds of night.[41]
- Fill the whole world with heaven's peace.[42]
- Pilgrim through this barren land.[43]
- Be though still my strength and shield.[44]
- Thy grace has made us strong.[45]
- By his love constraining, by his grace divine.[46]

- Grant us wisdom, grant us courage, for the facing of this hour.[47]

- Lost in wonder, love, and praise.[48]

- Be still my soul, the Lord is on thy side.[49]

Listening to music relaxes my spirit and places me in the present moment. It helps me maintain perspective. Something about music stabilizes my equilibrium.

CARRIED BY THE FAITH OF OTHERS

During the desert times of this uncertain journey, my spiritual health has been carried by the faith of others who have prayed for and with me. Friends have encouraged me with reminders that God is present in my confusion and that, though these may seem like uncharted waters to me, they are not to God. These friends have entered deeply into my world, and my heart is filled with gratitude. It's been a different position for me, as often I have been the one who encourages others. I am humbled and feel deeply loved.

One friend reminded me that my health diagnosis is really the ultimate test of my faith, and that I have been preparing a lifetime for this moment. Who am I, who will I be, how will I respond to adversity, and how does my faith shape or inform that?[50]

Another friend wrote the following to encourage me:[51]

The Spirit of the Lord says, "It is with joy I sing over you. I will uphold you with my righteous right hand. Your days are in my hand. I will fulfill the number of your days. I have put my spirit within you, a closeness only you understand. I have desired for you to be a light to the nations. Walk forth, not by might nor by power, but by my Spirit says the Lord.

Despite knowing that many love me, this journey is emotionally lonely, and my emotions affect my ability to find hope, experience optimism, and center myself on God.

SOAKING IN NATURE

I have found that nature calms my spirit. At times, I have watched videos of peaceful natural scenes. Other times, walking in the woods or by the stunning beauty of water has helped center me. They allow me to realize I am part of a much larger story.

While driving back to Seattle along the Pacific Coast after my 50th high-school reunion in Southern California, I stopped in Brookings, Oregon to visit a good friend from college. The morning after I arrived, I walked for an hour on the isolated beach. The waves rhythmically and endlessly crashed onto the sand, and I admired large rocks and cliffs that had been there for millennia. The walk centered my spirit as I absorbed the grandeur of God's amazing creation.

CHAPTER 20

SUBMISSION

Faith is our rock, not just when life is going well,
but also when our world is upended.[52]

Mike Purdy

While I always have understood theologically that God numbers our days, cancer has made this understanding very personal. God doesn't just number "our" days; he numbers and knows "my" days. God knows our beginning and our end, and he is present in all the moments in between.

Even in my sadness, I have hope because I know that God loves me, and even death will not separate me from his love. In a strange way, the invading tumors in my body are a friend, reminding me at a deep level of my calling that I belong to my faithful Lord and Savior in body and soul … and in death. As the Apostle Paul wrote, "Whether we live or whether we die, we are the Lord's." (Romans 14:8). Since I met Jesus more than a half-century ago, I have tried to live my life under his Lordship. Why should now be any different?

I remind my soul, "Fear not—for God holds you in his loving hands."[53] I try to surrender and submit myself to him. Living with a diagnosed uncertainty is a challenge but maybe it is helping me to live more fully. Maybe it is preparing me for the next journey of my soul.

So, I try to live my days in submission to him who loves me, even as my body is failing, and my emotions are all across the board. We are brought into existence by the love of the Creator. We don't own these bodies. We are entrusted with them for this temporal journey. At a deep level, though I live imperfectly, I long for my heart to be in tune with God's heart.

Despite the depth or length of our years we all will die when God ordains the end of our earthly pilgrimage. As we live these relatively short years in bodily form, we strive for health and healing and for making an impact. We struggle, however, with accepting the reality of our certain death. May we learn to be wise as we live fully in the here and now, knowing our time-bound days will end before we have accomplished and experienced all we long for.

CHAPTER 21

HEAVEN

There are better things ahead than any we leave behind.[54]

C.S. Lewis

As I confront the reality my body is being squeezed by out-of-control cells, I have thought a great deal about what comes after I breathe my last breath and my body returns to dust. The short answer is that I don't know. None of us knows with any certainty, so my observations here are speculations based on what I know about the created order of nature and the character of God.

In a mysterious way that I don't understand, heaven is simply a different form, a different plane of existence, a transformation from physical bodies into a new and different reality. "There is a fine dance between non-physical and the physical," wrote one friend. "We are asked to think in one dimension while at the moment we live in the other!"[55]

God created us as flesh-and-blood creatures on this earth, firmly planted in the here and now, inextricably bound by time and space. All we know now is the time and space in which we live. It's all we have experienced.

The day will come when time ceases to exist for us. Author Frederick Buechner expresses this poetically:

Time, like the receding waters of the ocean, bears all of us who are time's children farther and farther away from the near shore and closer and closer to those mysterious depths where we will come finally to our time's end.[56]

I am convinced that the world to come will be better and that the tragic impacts of sin and the brokenness of this world will evaporate. The beauty of nature as we experience it will be even more exquisite in the next world. It is hard, however, for us to imagine a different form of existence than the physical bodies and world that we inhabit.

Although we know that our mortal bodies one day will cease to function, we constantly deny this reality. We try to shove death under the carpet, and we do not recognize the elephant in the room that should help frame our lives as we strive to live well in the moment.

In one sense, I sometimes view death as a failure, that it shouldn't happen and that if only I were to act differently, I could escape it. Such thinking is ridiculous, of course, but I somehow expect or hope that my life and the lives of those I know will continue endlessly.

We have to face, however, the natural cycle of life. We are born and grow up, we live and love, we laugh and cry, we experience hope and fear, we marry and have children, we work and create, we grow old, and we leave this earth for the next phase of our existence.

Perhaps a parallel arises between childbirth and our twilight years. Pregnancy lasts for nine months, allowing a couple to eagerly prepare for and anticipate the arrival of a new life. Maybe my years of deteriorating health are a pregnancy in reverse. The time since I was diagnosed has allowed me to emotionally process my pending transition as I wind down the life I have been given. It also gives me space to anticipate the coming transformation.

God created us for eternity, even though we live but short lives on this planet. Our bodies are both amazingly durable and fragile. Our built-in expiration dates differ widely for each of us.

The unknown often fills us with fear and dread. We don't know what to expect and whether our experience will be good or bad. Death and heaven are the ultimate unknowns for human beings. Will we cease to exist, or will heaven be a far better experience than anything we have experienced or imagined?

Transitions in earthly life are often challenging. My 6-year-old grandson, Michael, struggles with them, perhaps because he so completely lives in the moment. If you ask him if he wants to go anywhere, such as the park or the zoo, he might stubbornly say no, even though he has had plenty of fun experiences in such places. He resists change just as we all resist the change that will come with the ultimate transformation from our physical existence on this earth to a new and unknown experience after death.

I certainly don't understand God's mysterious purposes and why amazing and full lives on earth come to an end. Why don't good people live longer, and evil people live shorter lives? Where is the rhyme or reason for the length of our days? Regardless, I trust that God loves me and his creation far more than I can fathom and that he will bring new life to me in a transformed and unknown world.

FORETASTE OF HEAVEN

When I drove back to Seattle along the Pacific Coast from my 50th high school reunion in San Marino, California in July 2022, I stopped to stretch my legs in the historic town of Port Orford, Oregon. A beautiful vista and a short path through dense shrubbery prompted me to take a walk. The strong fragrancy of flowers along the path filled my spirit. I paused in the moment to soak in this good experience.

I imagine that far more pleasing fragrances will fill heaven. As I breathed in the Oregon coastal flowers, I wondered whether smells are a foretaste of heaven. Since God has gifted us with the sense of smell, he has let us appreciate such delicacies. On morning walks each summer, I look forward to stopping to sniff honeysuckle and lilac blossoms.

Certainly, heaven will overflow with experiences unimaginably vivid. Earthly experiences, by contrast, are but a scant reflection and distant dream of the reality of the world to come. In C.S. Lewis' *The Last Battle*, the final book of the Chronicles of Narnia series, Lewis refers to life on earth as "the Shadow-Lands."[57] He describes the transformation for the main characters of the books:

> And for us this is the end of all the stories, and we can most truly say that they all lived happily ever after. But for them it was only the beginning of the real story. All their life in this world and all their adventures in Narnia had only been the cover and the title page: now at last they were beginning Chapter One of the Great Story which no one on earth has read: which goes on forever: in which every chapter is better than the one before.

In the same way, we are wired at the core of our existence to appreciate and affirm love, joy, peace, humor, and the beauty of the natural world. It's part of who we are. Our ability to savor these emotions and experiences affirms that we reflect the image of our Creator, who is all of these things in the purest form. In the world to come, I imagine we will realize how much our human experiences of good, however enjoyable, resemble an elusive shadow, a dim dream, bound by time and space. They are merely a foretaste of the life that is to come.

On a morning walk in late August 2022, the sun was at my back as it rose above Washington's Cascade mountains. Before me, I saw an exaggeratedly long shadow that made me seem taller and thinner than I am. Shadows are a strange phenomenon. We see them, but they are not tangible. We cannot hold onto or touch shadows. They vanish quickly, like our dreams.

The world we live in is but a shadow of the world to come. Perhaps we live in the Shadow-Lands, and heaven (or however we want to describe our existence after we breathe our last breath on earth), will be more real, vivid, and tangible than anything we've ever experienced.

In this world, if we're lucky, we are blessed with gentle and caring people whose actions reflect a deep expression of love. We breathe deeply to smell the fragrance of flowers. We marvel at the grandeur of majestic mountains and forests, of lakes and oceans, and find ourselves in awe as we stare into a dark night sky illuminated by the brightness of countless stars.

Yet all the good we experience in this life is perhaps just a shadow or foretaste of what is to come, and what will enfold us on that day when we are no longer bound by our 3D existence.

CREATED FOR CREATIVITY

God is the ultimate Creator. He breathes life into existence and "gives life to the dead and calls into being what does not exist." (Romans 4:17). Looking at the beauty and variety of people, plants, flowers, foods, and animals, I envision God's creative mind delighting in enthusiastically spinning new and unique things into existence: Venus fly traps; towering and massive Sequoia trees; exquisite orchids, fragrant lilacs, spherical dahlias, and romantic roses; some 8.7 million animal species, including peacocks with beautiful colored feathers, majestic bald eagles, and slithering snakes; artichokes, almonds, apples, and 400 different varieties of beans.

As humans, we are created in God's image and bear the mark of his creativity. Just as God takes pride in his creation, we take pride in the work of our imaginations and hands. We delight in the beauty of a garden we lovingly plant and tend. We eagerly enjoy a creative and tasty meal that we have prepared for the palate and presented to look colorful and beautiful.

We string together musical notes to create an array of types of music from classical music to jazz to juxtapose a unique set of sounds to please our ears. Maybe our creativity takes the form of woodworking or quilting or photography. For some, creativity emerges in their use of words to craft poetry, fiction, humor, or non-fiction.

My 6-year-old grandson has discovered hot-glue guns. He glues together bottle caps and other items, mined from the recycling container. A story and unique name accompany each creation.

The list of humanity's creative endeavors is limitless. We create in the same way that God's creative juices formed our world. He built his creative instincts into our core. So, it is only natural to expect an extension of creativity in the world to come.

Author and pastor Calvin Miller once wrote:

> Who can deny that your Maker made you to be a creator too? Whether you create things, ideas, relationships, scholarships, ideals, or concepts, you, like the God who fashioned you, are a maker.[58]

The Old Testament book of Genesis tells the story of how God created the heavens and earth. After the description of each element of his creation, we learn that God saw it was good. Here was the Creator being justifiably proud of what he had created. God has a vested interest and pride in his creation. He doesn't want his good creation of humankind to be extinguished at death, but he desires that it continue beyond this life. In this sense, it seems that God's delight in his creation supports the existence of life beyond the space and time by which we are bound on this earth. We don't know with any certainty what heaven will be like or in what form we will exist, but we have a reasonable assurance that when we breathe our last, our life will continue at a different level.

We see the renewal of life built into nature by the Creator as we observe flowers and plants. They begin from mere seeds. Initially, there is no bud, emerging flower, or blossom. Yet as surely as one spring fades and flowers fall, in another flowers bloom afresh the next spring. Creation is renewed by the hand of the infinitely creative God.

In one sense, we as humans follow a similar pattern. Newborn babies grow to toddlers, then young children, to teenagers and finally to adults. Just as flowers die and grow again, so, too, we die and will one day be resurrected to new life. What form our new form will take remains a mystery. God is the God of creation, and certainly there will be new life for people who he loves infinitely more than animals, flowers, and plants.[59]

I realize that my life on this swirling mass of land and water orbiting the sun is part of God's eternal plans and that a new and glorious future awaits me after my earthly pilgrimage is done. This assurance should make it easier for me to deal with the sadness, loneliness, and grief I experience as I contemplate the end of my journey here, and as I experience the demise of my dreams and what it means to live with unmet expectations. Amid struggles and sin that easily consume me, my deepest desire is that my heart remains close to God's heart. In the words of one hymn, we are "ever singing, march we onward, victors in the midst of strife."[60]

WHO WILL BE IN HEAVEN?

Christian theology teaches that salvation and entry to heaven is reserved only for those who confess Jesus as their Lord and Savior. However, legitimate questions arise about what happens to people who have never heard of Jesus. Likewise, is a simple confession sufficient or must one live his or her life a certain way after such a confession? Clearly, who will enter heaven is a complicated topic. The truth is, we simply don't know. God has not revealed this to humanity with certainty or specificity. It's ultimately in his hands.

Thus, given the uncertainties, I prefer to be agnostic about how to answer the question.

Just as we are proud of our continuing creative enterprises and we want our creations to endure, the Creator is proud of what he has created, not just the galaxies, the universe, and this planet but also every detail of creation, including and especially human beings who are created in his image—of you and me. Put simply, we reflect his creativity.

Since God is proud of his unique creation, why would he relegate his creation to the dustbin of history after our earthly journey is over? Would he not want his good creation to endure, just as we want the good work of our creative hands and minds to last? Whatever we are transformed into when we pass from this life to the next, we will continue to reflect the image and creativity of God.

Relationships are at the core of our human existence. Because what we experience on earth is but a dim reflection of what is to come, I suspect we will enjoy relationships much more deeply than anything we experience here and with a wide variety of people, simply because God is a god of relationships.

I'd like to reconnect with or meet anew many people in heaven. Of course, I hope to see my parents and people I have known who have since crossed the great divide. In heaven, I also would love to get to know giants of the faith whom I have respected and learned from at a distance including the Apostle Paul, Saint Augustine, Martin Luther, John Wesley, William Wilberforce, Dietrich Bonhoeffer, Charles Finney, Dwight Moody, C.S. Lewis, Billy Graham, Charles Simeon, Polycarp of Smyrna, Mark Hatfield, John Stott, Frederick Buechner, and hundreds more.

Ultimately, I believe God is just and fair, and whatever his judgment on individuals and who enters heaven will be fair and just, and each person will agree with that judgment, whatever it is. We simply don't have enough information about who will and will not be in heaven.

HISTORIANS IN HEAVEN

I have loved history since I was a young boy. As an 8-year-old in Princeton, New Jersey, I memorized the names of all the presidents in order of service from pictures of them I taped to my bedroom wall. I voraciously read most of the biographies in my elementary-school library. I read and collected articles about events in American history and kept them in my wooden "history box." I typed up a list of the names of famous people about whom I knew something. On weekends with my dad, I visited historical sites, such as where George Washington crossed the Delaware River on a bitterly cold Christmas Day, and the Princeton Battlefield.

History captivates me. I love reading about what life was like in times past. It's fun to research facts and use my imagination to understand historical events. What was the nature of relationships people had with each other? What emotions did they experience? How can I recreate the past?

I have always wanted to document my own history, whether writing in my journal or making calendar notes about what I did each day. I deluded myself into thinking that someday someone might care about reading about my schedule, but even if not, the calendars help me remember how I used my hours.

After my mom, brother, and I moved to Southern California from New Jersey when my mom and dad divorced, I typed on index cards the addresses to which our family moved and the dates of moving in and moving out. What 10-year-old does that? An appreciation of history seems to be at my core.

My love of history led me to hang up my shingle as a presidential historian in 2014 despite having no degree in history. I did this with only a love for history and knowledge derived from decades of reading. I have been fortunate to write two books about the presidents. I have been interviewed by national and international media outlets about presidential history and politics. I have written articles for online publications.

When this earthly body finally gives way to dust, what will happen to my love of history in the world to come? I hope I will be able to interact with presidential historians and famous people who have preceded me. Maybe there will be a need for historians in heaven.

If history is part of my core, perhaps my love of history will continue and carryover into heaven as I'm in a different form. Maybe I will be able to continue to do things that I want to do.

My hope is that my essence as a person will continue after death, which is simply a transformation to a different form. These, of course, are difficult things to know, and the unknown often brings fear to our hearts.

RELATIONSHIPS IN HEAVEN

Death and heaven are not an end but the beginning of a new form of existence that we have trouble fully understanding. Even so, we can rest confidently that it will follow the pattern of life, death, and rebirth that we observe in the creation of this world.

Certainly, God is a God of relationships. He is a relational Creator who desires a living relationship with his creatures just as parents invest a lifetime in developing relationships with their children. Relationships are foundational in God's economy. In the here and now, we long for emotional intimacy, and our spirits thrive in warm and convivial relationships. We long to be known deeply by others, just as we desire to know others deeply. We walk with others on their journeys as they walk with us. We share our story and listen to the stories of others. In the next phase of our existence, we will have an eternity of opportunities to continue those stories, to nurture old relationships and build new ones.

My biggest source of sadness as I contemplate an end to my ever-narrowing days is that I will miss family and dear friends I have been privileged to know, and who have walked with me on the journey of life. I don't want that to end. I don't want to leave them alone without me. Yet I know that is the course of human existence. It doesn't change my sadness. It is comforting, therefore, to imagine and hope for the continuation and deepening of relationships in heaven.

With my love of history, I imagine that I may encounter ancestors who will fill in gaps of my knowledge about what their lives were like before my time.

Somehow God has wired us to be relational as he is relational. Maybe that's a major part of what it means to be created in his image.

Certainly, heaven will feel better and be far richer than a family or class reunion and will teem with affirming relationships and deep connections that will fill our souls. We will be known deeply by our Creator and others, and we will see and know clearly. "Beloved, we are God's children now; it does not yet appear what we shall be, but we know that when he appears we shall be like him, for we shall see him as he is." (1 John 3:2).

HOME AT LAST

There is something deeply embedded in our psyche about wanting to be at home, to experience a place of total acceptance and love. For some people, the home they grew up in provided a grounding influence and stabilizing point. Unfortunately, for others, the home of their early years did not represent an enriching or safe experience.

As we become adults, we seek to create our own homes—a new sense of community. We may live with families, friends, or by ourselves. Embedded deep within us is an image, faded or sharp, of what home should be like. Sadly, the homes we try to create do not always turn out as we had hoped. Home may become a place filled with stress, or even emotional or physical abuse. In our hearts, however, we always long for a safe refuge and a place of peace.

In due time, we will all be called home from our journey on this planet, from whatever type of homes we have experienced and created to the perfect home. It will be the final homecoming, one far deeper and richer than any earthly home, reunion, celebration, or holiday where we will see reality with perfect clarity.

Our earthly image of home is but a dim shadow of the perfect home, filled with peace, beauty, and warm and deep relationships. In that perfect home, we will be free to be ourselves, feel accepted for who we are, and be understood for who we are. Loneliness and relational strife will become a distant memory.

What makes the three-dimensional world we now inhabit so challenging at times is that it is the only world we know or at least the only existence we consciously remember. Thus, we cling to it, even though the truth is we are just passing through this life before returning to our ultimate home.

This reminds me of words the Apostle Paul wrote to the church at Corinth: "We are of good courage, and we would rather be away from the body and at home with the Lord. So whether we are at home or away, we make it our aim to please him." (2 Corinthians 5:8).

CHAPTER 22

DREAMS

In the night also my heart instructs me.

Psalm 16:7

I often have wondered about the connection between heaven and the earthly dream world. Both are beyond what we can rationally or consciously understand. We experience our dreams, but we can't explain them, and we have trouble remembering them. They represent an altered state of consciousness. Are they a mysterious window into the reality of heaven?

I don't remember most of my dreams, and the ones I do remember often are nonsensical. If I try to describe a dream to someone, I feel like I am spouting gibberish, even though the feeling from the dream is still with me and makes sense. It's hard to find words to describe a dream.

If we have trouble remembering our dreams when we awake each morning, perhaps in the new reality of heaven—in our new existence—our memories of life on earth will be similarly clouded.

In the words of Aslan from C.S. Lewis' *The Last Battle*, we live now "in the Shadow-Lands," which is our only reality until the day our pilgrimage here on earth is done. This world is but a shadow or dream of what is to come.

In some mysterious way, God uses dreams to speak to us. As the Old Testament Psalmist notes, from, in, and through our dreams, God uses them to "instruct" us. Dreams can be delightful journeys into joy and peace, terrifying rides through fear and horror, or simply a jumble of unexplained and often bizarre experiences. When I awake, sometimes I feel a deep feeling in my heart of being loved, or I feel a sense of weight as though my dreams were deeply troubling. My hope and prayer is that somehow God will speak to my heart and encourage me not only at night but also in the daytime.

When we lie down to sleep, we relinquish control of our body and spirit. Thus, going to sleep each night is an act of faith while our body is in slow motion and hibernation, and our spirit enters the dream world where anything can happen. It is during this time that we turn to God to hold us and speak to us.

On Feb. 23, 2022, I received an unusual Facebook Messenger text from a stranger. It read as follows:

Hello! My name is Christine. I realize this may sound strange; however, I must ask, are you looking for a transcriber or typist? I had a dream in which your full name appeared, so I searched Facebook, and low and behold, here you are. If you are looking for clerical type of assistance, I can send you more information about myself.[61]

My first thought was that must be a scam. I was skeptical about such an out-of-the-blue and mystical message. I was tempted to ignore it, but I also was intrigued.

While I believe that God can speak to us in dreams, especially if we're spiritually sensitive, this story was far outside my comfort zone. I have not had an experience quite like this.

In the book of Job in the Old Testament, we read the following:

For God speaks in one way and in two, though man does not perceive it. In a dream, in a vision of the night, when deep sleep falls upon men, while they slumber on their beds. (Job 33:15-16).

I decided to not dismiss Christine's message out of hand. I looked her up on Facebook since that is the platform she used to contact me. I watched a video she had posted of her reading from scripture and singing. She seemed genuine and a person of deep faith.

I shared this unusual situation with family and friends to get their opinions. Most people encouraged me to respond, although a few were adamantly suspicious and were convinced it was a hoax.

I decided to reply. I sent Christine a message stating, "I do believe God speaks to us in our dreams, if only we are able to remember them as they vanish so quickly. I don't really know what to make of your message, but I want to be open to God's leading." She agreed: "It's obvious the Lord is up to something we don't yet understand."

Curiously enough, I did have a variety of pieces I have written over the years that I wanted to have typed that didn't get included as part of assembling my four volumes of selected writings that I self-published in 2021 under the title *Grace in the Wilderness: The Heart and Mind of Mike Purdy*. In addition, I had done radio and television interviews on presidential history and politics with national and international media outlets, and I wanted them to be transcribed so they could be preserved in written form. Due to the press of other things, I hadn't taken the time to try to locate someone to type these documents.

Christine and I agreed to meet via a Zoom call. When we talked, she shared how she heard my name audibly in her dream and said it was crystal clear. She woke up and wrote my name down. She told me the story of how COVID-19 has financially stressed her family, as she and her husband lost their jobs.

We agreed I would assign her some documents to type or transcribe using a well-known online freelance website for the assignments and payments. She has done good work, and I have paid her for her services. Since then, she has started her own business and hasn't been available to continue typing documents for me.

How should I interpret this unusual situation? It's clear that Christine's offer to type documents was not a scam. Could she have researched people on Facebook and sent the same message to multiple people with the same story? That is possible, but I sense that she was being honest and that it would be out of character for her to do that. The final possibility is that God spoke to her in a dream. Her spiritual sensitivity supports that.

Having Christine reach out to me encouraged my heart. My unexpected health challenges have taken me down a lonely and dark path filled with rocks and tree roots on which to stumble, and at times I have felt God has abandoned me. Perhaps God hasn't deserted me after all. He used Christine's dream to remind me that he has not forgotten me and that there is a real world beyond our physical reality.

COMPANIONS FOR THE JOURNEY

CHAPTER 23

DEEPENING FRIENDSHIPS

Be with people who are good for your soul.

I dedicated my book, *Presidential Friendships: How They Changed History*, to my friends. Here's what I wrote:

> To my friends of a lifetime as well as more recent ones,
> near and far, who have walked with me on this joyful,
> sometimes tearful, and uncertain journey of life.
>
> You have enriched my life with your prayers, love,
> encouragement, humor, wisdom, empathy, and support.
>
> I've been privileged to walk with you as well in the
> various seasons and situations of your lives.
>
> That's what good friends do.
> We make a difference for each other.

I am grateful and blessed to be surrounded by these friends, these companions for the journey, who have sustained me in difficult times.

As then Vice President George H.W. Bush wrote, "You see, friends make everything better."[62] He surely was right.

In an unexpected way, the rogue cells ravaging my body have brought heartfelt joy and deepened my friendships far beyond what I could have anticipated. This rich season of life has brimmed with the love and affirmation of friends who often listened to me as I tried to process my mortality. Sometimes I have teared up or cried uncontrollably, but friends have multiplied my joy and divided my pain so that I am not bearing it alone.

Being surrounded by friends reminds me that none of us walk this rocky path alone. We all are interconnected. To be human is to recognize our interdependence. The poet John Donne famously wrote, "No man is an island."[63] I am accompanied on this sometimes-arduous hike by many dear friends who have held my hand, provided valuable and insightful perspective, and offered tangible means to support me. These friendships have been a source of immeasurable encouragement and sanity for me on this often sad and lonely journey as I contemplate the end of my days. I have been touched by the loving care, support, and encouragement of so many good friends. It's really been very sweet.

Two months after I was diagnosed with metastatic prostate cancer, I wrote in my journal about how friends had been there for me: "I have been very touched and felt loved and supported by so many friends in response to this cancer and their enthusiasm and rejoicing with me over the new PSA score." On July 12, 2019, when I wrote those words, I had just received positive news about a significant decrease in my PSA based on the hormone-therapy injections that were reducing my testosterone and starving the cancer.

Friends have been present to both rejoice and to cry with me. Plenty of times, my PSA has gone up or a scan has shown increased cancer growth. I have felt supported and loved by so many dear friends who have wept with me.

CHAPTER 24

NO REGRETS

At the end of the day, let there be no excuses, no explanations, no regrets.

Steve Maraboli
Life, the Truth, and Being Free

At the end of my days on this planet, I don't want to have any regrets about what I have said or not said to my companions on this grand adventure of life. Have I held back speaking honestly and lovingly with others about the past, the "what-ifs" of life, or my feelings of love, appreciation, and gratitude for them in the present moment? I have tried to be deliberate in writing or speaking candidly. I try to live each day with complete and loving honesty, knowing that my present time evaporates into history ever too quickly, and that I don't know when I might see or talk with anyone again. I don't want to reach the point where I say to myself, "If only I had said" something to a loved one. There's no moment like the present, and we are given only the present moment.

In July 2022, I embarked on a 3,000-mile road trip from my home in Seattle to Southern California for my 50th high-school reunion and then back during which I visited family and friends. As I talked with and hugged people and said goodbye to them, I knew that these hugs and chats could represent the last time I see them in this life. Those were sobering moments. I tried to take a snapshot in my mind of those significant encounters.

I want to have told those close to me how much they mean to me. Why should I wait to love and express love? Swiss philosopher, mystic, poet, and critic, Henri Frederic Amiel wrote in the 1800s:

> Life is short and we have never too much time for gladdening the hearts of those who are travelling the dark journey with us. Oh be swift to love, make haste to be kind.

I am so blessed with people who love me. I recently began calling some friends on their birthdays. I am all too aware that this could be my last time talking with them in this life, and I don't want to let that opportunity escape.

In these twilight years, I try to be deliberate about each decision and the use of my time, knowing my days are shrinking. I don't want to operate out of fear or regret. I don't want to fritter away the moments I have been gifted. In order that I may pass well from this world, I try to live well each day as though it were my last.

CHAPTER 25

CULTIVATING FRIENDSHIPS

Friendship is the only cement
that will ever hold the world together.[64]

Woodrow Wilson

When I was a young boy and emerging adult, I thought of myself as an intro-vert, though that may not have been wholly accurate. As I grew older, I saw myself more an extrovert, or at least a healthy balance between introversion and extroversion. Nevertheless, I don't think I did enough to cultivate friend-ships, especially among work colleagues.

During the years when I focused on pursuing a career, raising two kids, and getting a seminary degree (all at the same time!), I felt I didn't have much spare time to build friendships. I was exhausted and stretched thin. I have acquaintances from those years with whom I wish I had kept in touch with, but I was at maximum capacity with very little margin in my life for others. In those days, of course, social media didn't exist and so it wasn't as easy to cement a connection into cyberspace.

I held many work colleagues at arm's length and didn't allow some of those relationships to morph into friendships. I think I was some-what stand-offish at times. Perhaps I responded in that way due to feeling overwhelmed with life, or I thought I should keep separate my professional and personal lives. I am grateful, though, that years removed from the workplace, I have reconnected with some colleagues and have begun to establish rewarding friendships.

When I retired and moved into consulting, I began to make more friends, both among clients and former colleagues. I think the main reason is that I felt I had more space in my life. Our kids were launched, more or less, I didn't have to punch a time clock, and I was done with seminary.

Recently, Ginny, a friend from the world of public contracting and procurement organized quarterly Zoom happy hours for former colleagues from my days as a consultant and trainer. The purpose of this group, whose membership waxes and wanes, is to come together in community and sharing, and also to hear updates on my health. I have found some of these sessions emotional, and at times I have wept while sharing the reality of my difficult situation. While I have felt supported and loved by the others, I also hope my candid sharing might be a source of reflection and encouragement for others as they face their own mortality.

I realize how incredibly important friends are for the challenging journey I find myself on as I contemplate the end of my days. I feel blessed to grow old with dear friends. But sometimes having people love me deeply has been hard. I don't feel like I deserve it, as though somehow I must earn the love of others. When attention is focused on me, I have felt guilty. While I have tried to show care for others, often the conversations are one-sided as I process what is happening to me physically, emotionally, and spiritually.

While, of course, I never would have chosen to be diagnosed with prostate cancer, my heart is nevertheless grateful beyond measure for how so many friendships have deeply enriched my life in ways that probably would not have occurred without my failing health. Sad as this disease is, I have experienced the love of others.

Friends have helped create an important sense of community for me as we share our common humanity. Certainly, COVID-19 has broken down community. From March 2020 until November 2022, I didn't worship at my church in Seattle in person. Services are now both in person and online, and I have only recently begun to periodically attend in person with a mask—in order to protect my compromised immune system.

In one sense, community is a spiritual discipline because God is a god of relationships. He values a relationship with us and is pleased when we are in a relationship with him and others of his creation.

I feel like I have lived a lifetime with friends since my diagnosis. These wonderful creations of God have stood with me, listened to me process life, wiped away my tears, given me permission to be human with my deep and confusing emotions, and allowed me to be vulnerable without judgment. They have offered their love, support, encouragement, and wisdom, and have prayed for me. They make me feel complete and ever so grateful. My heart is full.

CHAPTER 26

ROTATING FRIENDS

The better part of one's life consists of his friendships.[65]

Abraham Lincoln

I have noticed a mysterious and pleasant phenomenon in the years since my diagnosis. God seems to bring the right people into my life at just the right time. My circle of friends often seems to take carefully orchestrated turns, rotating through my life when I need them most. Just when I need someone to talk with, a person who I haven't talked with in a while contacts me. I am learning to trust God and listen to the wisdom each of these friends brings and what God may want to teach me through them.

Sometimes these friends will send or bring me a book. Likewise, I am growing to open myself to the fact that God may be speaking to me through the books, even though they might not be ones I would read immediately.

In addition to established friends, new friends have showed up in my life. Some have been unlikely candidates, entering my world in ways I never would have expected. But they have brought deep wisdom and perspective while supporting and encouraging my heart.

As I have recounted earlier, I met Christine, the typist, online when she responded to me after dreaming my name. She has been a source of godly encouragement, helping point my sometimes-distracted heart back to the God I love so dearly. She embodies what it means to be a friend who carries me with her faith and prayers when I am too weak and filled with physical and emotional pain. Many others consistently have done this for me as well.

Patricia graduated from my high school a few years after me. Even though I didn't know her back then, she invited me to be a Facebook friend, something I accepted and have done with others from my high school. At one point she posted a message about some of her struggles. I reached out to her via Messenger to encourage her. We have since met and continued to stay in contact, and with her positive thinking she has been a source of encouragement.

Donna was one of my high-school classmates, but I didn't know her well then. When she asked via Facebook why I had not posted recently, I shared with her and a few others details of my condition. As a result, Donna graciously "adopted me." She has been diligent and consistent in checking in with me via text almost every week. Her genuine caring has deeply touched my heart. She has made me feel that I am not forgotten as I hike this sometimes-rocky path up a steep mountain.

In late October 2020, in the mail came an anonymous postcard wishing me well. The sender wrote, "A little bird told me, 'I think Mike could use a little extra positive input right now.' So, you've been added to my early morning meditations now. Power. Daily healing light. Hang in there, friend." It was signed "Peace," but with no name. The next day, another one arrived, also ending with "Hang in there, friend" and "Peace." For a while, these postcards arrived almost daily. Then there were lulls. But over nearly two years, I received close to 40 such postcards.

Most of the postcards were older, and their stamps were unusual. Sometimes, the messages recounted facts about what was depicted on the postcard's face, as well as encouraging words. I was stumped. I didn't know anyone in the California city where most of them were postmarked.

In early July 2022, I attended my 50th high school reunion in San Marino, California. At an informal get-together, I had just parked my car at the high school and was walking to a courtyard when a classmate, Michael, drove up. We chatted for a minute while he was still in his car. He said we would continue talking after he parked. When he got out of his car, he handed me a postcard with the same handwriting as the others with the "Peace" sign-off and a note: "So glad you made it for the 50th. Hang in there." I had discovered my mystery well-wisher.

I first met David when I was a consultant and taught a class on government construction contracting. During a break, David asked my help on a major school-remodeling project for which he served as project manager. I worked with him on that and other projects. Over time, our professional relationship became a friendship, and he has continued to be supportive of me. He periodically texts or calls me. Once, in mid-March 2022, he texted me to see how I was doing and asked when I could talk. I gave him days and times including the present moment. He called immediately and we talked for 75 minutes.

I met Susan at the 2018 Presidential Sites Summit in Washington, DC when she sat down next to me at a breakfast round table. We struck up a conversation and talked at other times during the conference. When I visited Washington the following year while sightseeing with my son, I joined Susan one evening for appetizers. We have continued to stay in touch. Just before Christmas 2020, we talked by phone. She said my voice was strong, something many people have said. Of course, these were times when I was not breaking down and weeping. More important, she reminded me that Dec. 21 was the darkest day of the year and wished that my health prognosis would only get lighter and better, just as the seasons change. That message of hope stuck with me a long time. We continue to talk by the phone.

This list of rotating friends is far from complete. In addition, 10 close friends have walked regularly with me at a deep level, many every day. They have encouraged me and listened to my words and sobs. I am indebted to these amazing people God has brought into my life.

CHAPTER 27

FRIENDS EASE LONELINESS

As for the saints in the land,
they are the noble, in whom is all my delight.

Psalm 16:3

Years ago, I was studying in the library of the local community college just a few miles from my house in Seattle. I was there to find quiet to focus on reading theology for my seminary classes. Snow had accumulated outside on that cold day, with temperatures in the 30s. As I looked out the library window, I watched students walking between classes, some side-by-side in animated conversation. Others walked alone. I was struck at that moment by how we all long for connection and conversation with others. I felt sorry for those walking alone, hoping they had significant people in their lives.

I don't like to be alone, especially as my body fails and I face the unknown. In many ways, my journey is solitary. My body endures the needles, scans, infusions, injections, medications, side effects, and appointments, but fortunately, my dear friends walk with me, sometimes daily, helping make my journey less lonely.

We are created for relationships and community and not to walk alone. Without companions for the journey, we tread through the dark valley of loneliness. Relationship and community are innate parts of our humanity. Unfortunately, loneliness is all too prevalent and a tragic consequence of humanity's brokenness.

The COVID-19 pandemic that changed our world in March 2020 created isolation as we retreated to the safety of our homes. With chemotherapy, my immune system is compromised, and I have had to take extra precautions to stay healthy. That has meant fewer social interactions in person. The world of friends has not been what it might have been in a non-pandemic world. Nevertheless, I am grateful for the support I have received from friends by text, email, phone, and some limited outside get-togethers.

Toward the end of July 2022, I was depressed about the state of my deteriorating health and my rising PSA. I talked and cried that morning by phone with a friend as I processed the seeming unfairness of my situation. Recent news from my oncologist filled me with renewed dread as the doctor shared that chemo probably was not working and that I would need to use up yet another of my limited options available. While feelings of dread and deep sadness remain, I felt comforted by my friend.

We are all getting older, and my life always will be unfinished. Yet somehow, I resolve to press onward in faith, knowing that God walks with me.

CHAPTER 28

TANGIBLE TOKENS

Let us be grateful to people who make us happy.
They are the charming gardeners
who make our souls blossom.

Marcel Proust

Some tangible expressions of love and support go beyond words. Some friends have given me gifts. Others have walked with me through acts of service. They all humble me, especially when I feel I don't deserve to be loved in these ways.

I am reminded of Linus in the "Peanuts" comic strip who walks around clutching his security blanket. Blankets can be comforting. We wrap or cover ourselves with them. They can give us the feeling of being enfolded with the love of others.

Early on, my dear cousin Alex sent me a lightweight homemade quilt for me to use as I lay on the couch, perhaps exhausted from treatments or just needing an afternoon nap. Her thoughtfulness deeply touched my heart and I think of her every time I cover myself with the quilt, as if her love also covers me at that moment.

One day, a large package arrived from a high-school friend who had learned about my health challenge. It, too, was a beautiful handmade quilt, this one more for winter weather. Carol sent it as a tangible expression of support. I am grateful that she chose to share the fruits of her creative labor and talent with me.

A close friend from college, Cindy, surprised me by sending me a beautiful, warm and furry blanket. I love its soft feel against my face and think about our friendship as I lie on the couch covered by this additional tangible expression of support and love.

In anticipation starting chemotherapy and likely losing my hair, Cindy also sent me a warm and furry hat that I have enjoyed on cold Seattle mornings while walking. Mercifully, so far, I have not lost my hair, although I would gladly lose all of it if the treatments would arrest the spread of the cancer. My hair has thinned out, then grown back, then thinned out again, and it has definitely changed from a distinguished salt and pepper to old-man salt.

I am reminded each time I use the quilts, blanket, and hat that I am not alone on this journey. I think about these dear friends each time I cover myself with their kind gifts.

During the first year and a half of the pandemic, I was alone in Seattle while my wife was in Boise with our son and his family as she cared for our grandson, something she had done since shortly after he was born, when we lived in Alaska for three years. Originally, we had planned for me to be in Boise with the family and fly to Seattle when necessary for medical appointments. But with the rise of COVID-19, none of us thought it would be a good idea for me to fly, especially since my immune system was compromised due to the various treatments.

While it was a lonely time in some ways and I had to figure out how to fend for myself in preparing meals, I was not alone. Given my immune system, I avoided going to stores, so I relied on friends until I figured out the mechanics of grocery delivery. One neighbor regularly asked me what I needed whenever she went to Costco. Another friend also did Costco and Whole Food runs for me. A couple nearby regularly filled my orders for fruits and vegetables from a local produce stand and delivered them. A friend from church dropped by with vegetables from his garden. A couple from church delivered homemade soup. One friend I met on my morning walks loaned me a book and a Himalayan salt lamp.

Other friends, who know me (and my weakness) well sent me books! They ranged from inspirational to health-related to historical.

I have been the grateful recipient of these and other tangible expressions from friends as I have tried to maintain my bearings on this uncertain and arduous hike. I have depended on others for tangible kindness as well as words of encouragement and their physical presence.

CHAPTER 29

THE FIRE PIT

Friendship is one of the sweetest joys of life.
Many might have failed beneath the bitterness of
their trial had they not found a friend.

Charles Spurgeon

COVID and my compromised immune system have not produced a good formula for me to have face-to-face social interactions. This has spelled isolation. Even as much of our society begins to unmask, I have maintained a strict N-95 masking protocol when in public. Out of necessity, I have been cautious about being near people. The pandemic increased isolation and made it harder to connect.

Since the pandemic began, I have eaten inside with others (other than my family) on only five occasions, three of which took place during my 50th high-school reunion trip. I wore a mask the entire time except during the act of eating.

I miss face-to-face social interactions. While email, phone, and text are wonderful tools for staying in touch, they are a poor substitute for being in someone's presence and experiencing mutual tears and hugs, all things I need so much.

One day in December 2021, with Seattle temperatures not cracking 40 degrees, my wife and I entertained four friends (plus two children) on our back deck. To our surprise, one person brought a propane-powered fire pit they set up to keep us all warm as we enjoyed a meal and good conversation. We marveled at how warm the fire pit kept us while we maintained appropriate social distancing. Soon, this group chipped in and sent us our own fire pit.

Since then, we have made good use of the fire pit and have entertained others on the deck for meals. It has been good for my spirit to be in the physical presence of others other than my medical team.

In one sense, the COVID-19 shutdown made having a compromised immune system easier, but it has become harder as fewer people mask up and I continue to do so. However, I resolve to be cautious. The last thing I need is to contract COVID while my body tries to respond to treatments that will keep the cancer at bay.

CHAPTER 30

SUPPORT GROUPS

*Find kindred spirits with whom to share
the burdens of your journey.*

Mike Purdy

Many people going through health or other challenges in life find comfort and encouragement from those facing similar circumstances by taking part in support groups. Generally, I have avoided such networks because they seem depressing. One friend affixed the word "ick" to my experiences with such support groups.

Prior to COVID, I attended one session of a prostate-cancer support group in Seattle. Attending were 30 people, mostly men, along with spouses or significant others, all gathered on folding chairs in a circle in the basement of a community center. As a new attendee, I was asked to share my journey and treatments. Afterward, a medical professional spoke. I don't remember the topic.

I have remained on the mailing list for the group. For a while, all meetings were online due to COVID, then they switched to a combination of in-person and virtual. I went to one additional meeting when the topic was particularly relevant.

Certainly, I could learn from attendees and speakers, and maybe I'll go back someday. For now, however, the thought of attending such a group feels depressing. Maybe I just want to put my head in the sand and not think about my failing health, but to attend feels hopeless.

I feel the same way about four Facebook support groups for prostate cancer. While I picked up interesting information at times, reading the posts is an unwelcome reminder that I have a life-threatening illness without a cure.

I want to do what I can to promote my health, but I also don't want to spend all my time involved with these groups and chasing my health. I want live fully, doing life-giving activities to which I feel called. Finding the right balance is a challenge.

There is a sense in which actual, virtual, or social-media support groups disturb my spirit.

In the spring 2022, a cancer support group formed at my church, Bethany Presbyterian, in Seattle. Due to COVID and my still compromised immune system, I have attended online only. This group has felt different and more positive than others I have mentioned, perhaps because it includes the all-important spiritual dimension, and these are people I know and who know me.

MY JOURNEY REMEMBERED

CHAPTER 31

LEGACY

My days are like an evening shadow.

Psalm 102:11

I don't want to be forgotten when my existence in this life is over. I want to be remembered. The historian in me wants to ensure that the details of my life do not simply vanish upon my death but are preserved and that I leave a legacy that will endure long after I am gone. Maybe it's also a common human response that none of us want to be forgotten.

What have I accomplished in life? I hope I have made an impact and done significant things that will stand the test of time after my body gives out. I remember during my career as a contracting manager for government agencies that I wrestled with and wondered whether my daily work held significance and meaning. I wanted (and still want) my life to count, and to know that I have had a real, positive, and tangible impact on others.

While intellectually and theologically I know that real significance comes from the fact that I am significant to, and loved by God, I nevertheless want to be faithful in how I live my life and in following God's calling. I have been planted on this earth, in this time and place, to work in partnership with my Creator in building and nurturing lives. None of this understanding detracts from my personal desire that my life would be remembered by other people.

Perhaps I can take some small comfort in the words of our 23rd president, Benjamin Harrison, who wrote, "Great lives do not go out. They go on."[66] All of our lives are "great lives" full of complexity, wonder, and accomplishments. Harrison was addressing the concept of legacy. Legacy is about our lives continuing in some form after our pilgrimage on this planet is over.

With the rogue cells proliferating in my body, I have thought a lot about legacy and what it means to be remembered. I realize with sadness that less than 30 years from now the vast majority of my contemporaries, and even those younger, will have passed away. In two or maybe three generations at the most, I will be all but forgotten and merely a distant and dusty historical footnote. Virtually no one will have known or remembered me. It's a sobering thought. My two adult children will remember me. I also hope my now 6-year-old grandson will remember some things about me. It's doubtful, though, that I will live long enough for any great-grandchildren to know me.

Being diagnosed with cancer has hit me hard and positioned my mortality front and center in my world, despite my protestations that I somehow be entitled to a long life to have a greater impact. The reality is that whether I die now or later, I will die. It's not a question of if, but when. So, my desire is that I live well in the days I have, in the moments entrusted to me. I hope to leave a legacy and a positive and lasting imprint on this world.

However, my name will never be emblazoned in the history books for generations to come like those who have attained great fame or infamy. My life will not be known by generations yet to be born. I never will be famous, although I have a friend who playfully reminds me that I am already "rich and famous." Certainly, I have been blessed to write books and articles and be interviewed on radio and television. Perhaps my words may impact others and endure in some way.

My impact primarily will be indirect by trying to live fully and faithfully in the days entrusted to me. Perhaps my words or how I have treated people will help others to live well and be all that God has called them to be, giving them grace, confidence, and wisdom to treat their orbit of acquaintances with compassion and dignity. I hope for this ripple effect.

Is my desire to leave a legacy egotistical? Certainly, I admit part of me feels self-centered for wanting to leave a legacy. On the other hand, despite a selfish desire to be remembered, I think we should embrace and celebrate wanting to leave a legacy. Legacy is all about valuing a life co-created with God. He has walked with me each step of the way, and I have tried to turn to him. Thus, being concerned about my legacy is a way to honor God and his creation, and what he has done in and through me. It's a way for others to remember the faithfulness of God.

I may fret about whether I will leave behind a legacy, but the good news is that my Creator God will never forget me and that he is proud of his creation of me in this world.

Even God wants to be remembered. In the Old Testament, God asks that his people remember his faithfulness in practical ways and pass that onto future generations. He is concerned about ensuring his legacy endures. In Deuteronomy 6:4-9, we read the following:

> Hear, O Israel: The Lord our God is one Lord; and you shall love the Lord your God with all your heart, and with all your soul, and with all your might. And these words which I command you this day shall be upon your heart; and you shall teach them diligently to your children and shall talk of them when you sit in your house, and when you walk by the way, and when you lie down, and when you rise. And you shall bind them as a sign upon your hand, and

they shall be as frontlets between your eyes. And you shall write them on the doorposts of your house and on your gates.

As I have thought about legacy, I know I can have the most impact in three broad areas.

- The impact on lives I have touched
- The impact of my written words.
- The impact of my possessions that I pass along to others.

I want to be responsible in how I spend the days toward the end of my life. I want to love others and invest in them, to write as a means of extending my influence, and to give away meaningful possessions to those who will appreciate them.

At times, I feel frantic to pack in as much as I can into each day to accomplish these goals. I have to remind myself, however, that God who controls the timing of my departure, will give me time to do those things to which he has called me.

CHAPTER 32

LEGACY OF LIVES

The greatest legacy one can pass on … is …
a legacy of character and faith.

Billy Graham

I am under no illusion that I am living in the twilight years of my life. Perhaps, the sun will shine longer, as it does during warm summer days, or perhaps winter will bring twilight and darkness early. Regardless of the length of my days, the cancer enveloping my body has caused me to think about my priorities and what I sense God is calling me to in these days. Of course, that's something we should think about through all our years. Somehow, however, staring the likely end of life in the face has brought a fresh sense of reprioritizing.

One of my conclusions is that I want to invest in lives—people to love, listen to, encourage, counsel, and help. Extending my reach and influence through relationships and developing a legacy is something to which I feel deeply called in this season. This isn't to say I haven't always tried to do this. However, I feel a greater sense of urgency to connect with people and to pass onto them whatever I may have that might benefit them in their journeys. It's part of what I view as my legacy.

Our days are short to make a difference and leave a legacy. Our real impact comes from the lives in which we invest, with the hope that their lives will positively impact others. In the grand arc of history, our lives here are but a blip. Our bodies are not made for eternity, but our souls are. It is an interesting conundrum to have our spirits locked into these temporal bodies and experience the wide range of human emotions with which God created us.

NOT FORGOTTEN

Several dear friends have told me that they never will forget me and that my essence will live on in their hearts long after I am gone. My heart has been deeply touched by these expressions of love and appreciation. I am grateful I have touched their lives in some small measure.

For example, one friend wrote me, "You will be greatly missed by me and thousands of others whenever God transitions you to the non-physical. If we have not already transitioned, hopefully we will have learned by your example and will help others and carry on the good vibrations, wisdom, love, and joy."[67]

However, when I pass from this life, I will be just a memory for them, and this makes me sad. When they pass away, my direct influence on this world will evaporate, although perhaps whatever positive attributes and characteristics they might have picked up from me will, in turn, be passed onto others. My hope is that everything I do on this earth has a ripple effect not only here by indirectly impacting other lives, but also somehow in eternity. Touching hearts and lives and helping others grow is a high and joyful calling.

As one popular quotation on the internet notes:

Your impact on other people is bigger than you think. Someone still giggles when they think of that funny thing you said. Someone still smiles when they think of the compliment you gave them. Someone silently admires you. The advice you give has made a difference for people. The support and love you've offered others has made someone's day. Your input and opinions have made someone think twice. You're not insignificant and forgotten. Your existence makes a positive difference, whether you see it or not.

In "It's a Wonderful Life," the angel Clarence comments about the impact of individual lives to George Bailey, "Strange, isn't it? Each man's life touches so many other lives. When he isn't around, he leaves an awful hole, doesn't he?"

Sometimes we make a positive difference and don't even realize it. My friend, Laurie, once told me how much I have positively impacted her but then mysteriously said that she wouldn't ever tell me the details. I am left wondering but thankful.

Another friend from my morning walks, Tauri, has thanked me for being present with her during a particularly difficult season of her life.

WALKING THE JOURNEY WITH OTHERS

I enjoy walking with friends on their journeys, and I have been honored to be present as friends process broken marriages, depression, challenges with their adult children, health issues, loneliness, financial stresses, spiritual struggles, job hassles, and more. Being involved in the lives of others gives me a deep sense of fulfillment and purpose. It's part of my legacy of lives touched.

Of course, I am sad when I contemplate that my potentially short-ened days will deprive me of more opportunities to help others. I also worry about family and friends and pray God will provide them with others to meet their needs until the end of their journeys.

It has been fun and an honor to work with friends to strategize about their careers and mentor them. As one professional acquaintance wrote,

"It's not so much what you do; it's what you leave behind. It's how you develop other people with their careers; how you develop other people for new positions or to take your place."[68]

One gift that brings me deep fulfillment is when I use my skills at crafting words to benefit others. Writing comes naturally for me. I realize it doesn't come naturally for everyone, so when I can share my gift with others, it is an honor for me to help them. It's an important part of my legacy and how my life may be remembered.

I have drafted, revised, and polished multiple resumes, helped with job applications, coached friends on interview strategies, and even written graceful resignation letters. I have counseled friends on dealing with toxic work environments and how to "manage" their supervisors. I have been gratified when friends take my advice by starting to write weekly reports for their supervisors to improve communication and build their boss' confidence in them. I have served as a reference for many friends and colleagues in helping them obtain their next job.

I have enjoyed providing business and marketing advice to friends with small businesses or who want to start one. I have developed and written website content from bare-bone ideas and helped them brand their businesses.

I worked with one friend to write a description for marketing her house as an Airbnb. For another, I wrote a successful appeal letter for her to receive unemployment compensation.

Since my career involved writing and managing contracts, I have reviewed, edited, and written contracts for friends. I have written letters for friends to help them with contractual issues related to poor performance by construction contractors doing remodeling for their houses, as well as addressing rental agreements for houses. I wrote a letter for a friend to send to his former attorney to request the return of the unearned portion of a retainer he had paid them to handle an issue. The letter resulted in his recovering a significant amount of money.

Providing this free writing and consulting advice has been deeply satisfying for me, providing me with a sense of purpose and meaning. It has been a joy to help others in these ways.

In spring 2018, I chatted with the owner of the house across the street from us in Seattle. He mentioned he planned to sell his house soon. My son, David, and his family were living in Alaska, but I knew they wanted to move back to the Seattle area eventually to be closer to family. I suggested to my wife, Catherine, that we buy the house, rent it out, and have it available as a landing place for David and his family when they were ready to move. We bought the house before it went on the market and rented it out for about three years using a property-management company.

Fast-forward to fall 2021. David and his family were ready to move back to Seattle. They bought the house across the street from us and moved in. It has been heartwarming to have them living so close. I feel like I made a difference by suggesting we buy the house. Having my grandson across the street, especially as I have gone through chemotherapy and wrestled with my uncertain health, has brought joy to my heart. To spontaneously spend time with David and his family has enabled me to invest in their lives. It's part of my legacy to nurture relationships with future generations.

CHAPTER 33

LEGACY OF WORDS

You can make anything by writing.

C.S. Lewis

I am a writer at heart. I love writing and the process of creating vivid images and stories with words artistically arranged. Sometimes writing helps me to figure out what I think and feel, such as with my journal or this book. At other times, I write to communicate clear content, whether history, politics, theology, or business matters. Writing is an important part of my legacy and my ability to extend my reach and influence beyond the grave through books and other things I have written.

My dad was a high-school English teacher. As a result, through age 10, I grew up surrounded by literally thousands of books. That environment and my dad influenced me to similarly love books and words.

I remember that when I was 8, I wanted to write the definitive book about something. At that age, I started with a short story. I typed it, replete with plenty of misspelled words including the title. It was one of my few attempts in life at writing fiction. I entitled it "King Willam and the Duke of Lawrnce."[69]

In late June 2022, I went walking in the park with a dear friend of more than 20 years, Jennifer, who told me how much my words from preaching and leading worship services at church have meant to her. For many years, every Christmas Eve I was privileged to be the worship leader at the 8 p.m. candlelight service. I led the congregation through a meaningful welcome setting the context for our time together, reminded them of the meaning and significance of each week of Advent when we lit a candle (waiting, peace, joy, love), and led them into our time together with a call to worship, followed by a prayer inviting God's presence in that holy moment of our gathering together. From there, I read passages telling the Christmas story. In the final portion of my role as worship leader, I guided the congregation in a time of confession and prayer.[70]

Jennifer told me that listening to my words was the highlight of every Christmas for her, even more than presents or a Christmas meal. She said that she looked forward to Christmas Eve to hear my words in drawing the congregation into worship and reminding them of the significance of the season. I spent hours preparing my words for the Christmas Eve services and am grateful to know that my words resonated so deeply with her.

She similarly reminded me how meaningful to her were many of my words from sermons I preached at church, as well as words I used in teaching adult Christian education classes. Sometimes after I preached or taught, others also told me that they had been touched by what I had to say. Of course, I hope my words touched the lives of still others who didn't mention that to me.

When my mother-in-law passed away in 2006, the family asked me to conduct her memorial service. I was honored to craft the words for the service to honor and remember her 88 years of life. Similarly, when my 94-year-old father-in-law passed away seven years later, the family again turned to me to be the wordsmith and officiant. Neither of these events was easy but it was my privilege to help set the context for these lives and to remind the assembled family and friends that death reminds us, as nothing else does, of our mortality and frailty on life's journey.

On a more joyous occasion, in 2015, my niece by marriage asked me to officiate at her wedding. Even though I had graduated from seminary, I never pursued a pastorate and was not ordained. For the ceremony, I obtained ordination through an online organization that enabled me to officially conduct the ceremony consistent with the laws of Washington state. I enjoyed developing the words to make this special occasion a memorable one for all.

In 1994, after five years of pouring over untitled photographs, scraps of paper, diaries, and other memorabilia from my mom's life, I finished writing and published a biography of her life. While it is far from complete and more research remains, it felt good to pull together into one place various facts and weave them into the story of her life. Sadly, she passed away before I started the project and thus, she wasn't able to benefit from seeing the broad-brush strokes and themes of her life. Writing the book gave me a great sense of satisfaction to create something unique that could inform future generations about her life and times.

Over the years, I have conducted other family and genealogical research. The stories I reconstructed and documents I uncovered are important to me, and, I like to think, important to civilization in general. It makes me sad to not have more time to research and write.

In 2019, I published my first book about the U.S. presidents, following up on a lifelong passion and interest in our chief executives. The book is entitled *101 Presidential Insults: What They Really Thought About Each Other – and What It Means to Us*. Not only did I write the book to further establish my credentials as a presidential historian, but also because I saw it as an important part of my legacy. The book was the culmination of more than 30 years of reading and research during which I had collected quotations of presidents describing in uncomplimentary terms what they thought about other presidents. Beyond the collection of quotations, however, was my interest in arguing for a need for more civility in our public and private conversations, a subject I addressed in the book's introduction.

I was pleased and honored that a friend who runs a private philanthropic foundation was so impressed with the message about civility that he had the foundation buy and send a copy of the book to all members of Congress and to all 50 governors.

For me, words that reflect my thoughts and feelings are part of my legacy. In 2021, I finished a major project assembling and editing four large hardcover volumes totaling more than 2,600 pages of selected documents I have written over my lifetime. I entitled it *Grace in the Wilderness: The Heart and Mind of Mike Purdy (Selected Writings)*. Volume 1 deals with life and work. Volume 2 addresses family. The subject of Volume 3 is theology. Finally, in Volume 4, I assembled documents related to history and education.

When I was still a half year away from finishing my selected writings, I wrote in my journal about my motivation for embarking on such a massive project:

> Part of my sadness (or maybe fear) about an early death comes from my concern of not being remembered by people. Sure, I understand that life goes on after someone dies, and I wouldn't even want family, friends, and others to grieve over a long period of time but to get on with their lives. But I also don't want to be forgotten like I'd never lived or never impacted others. Perhaps that's why I'm so interested in publishing my selected writings—not that it will be a best seller or sold at all—but it will pull together in one place all of my writings to show the world (and me) that maybe I did accomplish something useful—that I was a thinker, and my writings can serve as a window into my mind and heart.[71]

I undertook editing and publishing my selected writings because I take great pride in a lifetime of writing. I knew that when I pass away, my uncollated writings most likely would have been recycled or thrown out. By publishing these pieces more formally, I hope that part of who I have been and what I have written will be preserved (the historian in me!) for future generations. I view these volumes as an important part of my legacy for family and friends.

In 2022, I published my second book on the presidents. It is entitled *Presidential Friendships: How They Changed History*. While I had intended the book to cover all presidential friendships, I decided that I didn't have sufficient time to write such a comprehensive book. Thus, the published book includes the stories of two pairs of friendships: between Theodore Roosevelt and William Howard Taft and between Franklin D. Roosevelt and Lyndon B. Johnson. Like my earlier presidential book, I wrote this one to follow my passion and published it to leave behind a legacy of a lifetime of my reading and research about the presidents.

I was asked to write and have written a book about government construction contracting issues. This important legacy project is the culmination of my more than 40 years of involvement with the subject, both as a contracting manager for government agencies and as an independent consultant. The idea was to share in a consolidated manner some of the knowledge I picked up over the years. I view this as an important legacy book and practical best-practices guide for a new generation of procurement and contracting leaders who are now in the workplace.

This book you are reading also is an important legacy I want to leave behind. Facing my mortality as I wrestle with the stark reality of cancerous cells running amok within my body has been a lonely journey in many ways. Certainly, I have had family and friends who have stood by me and walked with me. Ultimately though, it has been my journey alone. In writing this book, I hope to share with a broader audience some of what I have experienced so that others can learn how to face their own uncertain journeys and mortality with grace.

I have long lists of other books I want to write. I have enough for three lifetimes. It remains to be seen how many years God gives me, and how much additional writing I can still accomplish.

CHAPTER 34

LEGACY OF POSSESSIONS

Nothing you have not given away will ever really be yours.

C.S. Lewis

Over my lifetime, I have accumulated possessions that each tell a story about a season or moment in life. Some people discover they have too many things when they are preparing to move. I discovered it as I began to contemplate my diminishing days. Ultimately, such objects are not important, but for me they reflect choices of my life, spark memories, and embody images of what I have found important. Our stuff tells stories. Thus, it's important to me for people to appreciate my things and that I find appropriate homes for them.

Some people find it easy to dispose of such memorabilia. My sense of history makes it hard to throw some things out because they represent my history and lifetime.

In one sense, it seems silly for me to be preoccupied with making sure my possessions find good homes. After all, they are just inanimate objects: letters from friends or my parents, a high-school class ring, coins I have collected, books from my library, an award plaque from winning a high-school speech contest, family-history documents that have been passed onto me or that I have researched and developed. The list goes on.

Nevertheless, the historian in me, or maybe just the person who just doesn't want to be forgotten, hopes that significant items from my years will endure in some form after I have passed away. I don't want the memories of things that shaped and enriched my days to be tossed into a garbage can and my life forgotten and erased. I want to feel that my life somehow mattered and that some memories of me will endure. I also want future generations to be able to reconstruct part of what it was like to live in the mid-20th century and early 21st century. There are stories behind each item, and they bring color and detail to my days.

I now have more books in my house than a small library. In fact, my collection of books likely exceeds the number of books in the public library in Akron, Colorado, the small farming community in which I made my entrance into this world in 1954.[72]

Winston Churchill once wrote:

> If you cannot read all your books, at any rate handle, or, as it were, fondle them—peer into them, let them fall open where they will, read from the first sentence that arrests the eye, set them back on the shelves with your own hands, arrange them on your own plan so that if you do not know what is in them, you at least know where they are. Let them be your friends; let them at any rate be your acquaintances. If they cannot enter the circle of your life, do not deny them at least a nod of recognition.[73]

Books have been my friends over the years, with heavy concentrations of history and theology. One of my largest collections is of books about the U.S. presidents numbering about 750 volumes. What should I do with all these books? I would like them to be welcomed into a good home and appreciated. I am cataloging the books and have a tentative agreement with a university with a presidential-studies program to review the list and see which books to accept.

Other presidential books not wanted by the university I will offer to presidential historian friends. For example, I mailed a dozen books to a friend, Sharon, with whom I explored various presidential sites in Washington, DC, one day in the summer of 2018. She enjoys traveling to the historical sites, and the books will enhance her travels.

On Sept. 1, 2021, Hurricane Ida stormed the East Coast. Among the casualties were the offices of *American Heritage* magazine. They lost hundreds of books, magazines, and research files, including back issues of the magazine itself. I contacted the editor with a list of the issues of the magazine in my collection and mailed more than a 100 back issues of the magazine to replace what was damaged in the hurricane. It gave me great pleasure to know those magazines had gone home to where they belonged.

A good friend and rising leader from my days as a public contracting manager came by my house in summer 2021 to pick up contracting books from my library to help her career.

I mailed a dozen books about the history of Christian movements on college campuses to a long-time friend and staff member for InterVarsity Christian Fellowship.

I sent a box of language and editing books to an editor friend to enhance his library and help him in his career.

I hope to offer many of my theology books to good friends by offering them to come by the house and select what they would like. COVID-19 has delayed this project, but I hope it will happen.

I have started discussions with my children about memorabilia they want. Both Janet and David expressed interest in some things but sadly have no interest in other items. At one level, I understand this, but as one who is passionate about preserving history in all its forms, it's a difficult pill for me to swallow. Neither has the same level of interest in things that only have significance for me, nor do they have sufficient storage space.

My son, David, agreed to adopt a small bust of Abraham Lincoln I got from my dad. Of course, David has a history with it. After I packed it and shipped it from dad's house after he passed away, Abe got into some kind of altercation because he arrived in Seattle with a broken nose. Then an early teenager, David expertly repaired the plaster nose, and you can hardly see evidence of Abe's injury. David also agreed to provide a home for a gift my dad gave me: beautiful wood and metal bookends depicting The Thinker.

Janet expressed interest in a U.S. history textbook book that is one of the few possessions I took with me when my mom, brother and I moved from New Jersey to Southern California in 1964 upon my parents' divorce. She also is interested in an old analog clock I obtained when I was about 12 and delivering newspapers for the Los Angeles Herald Examiner. Part of my job was to sell subscriptions to the paper door-to-door. I earned enough points from sales to select this clock, which surprisingly still works after all these years.

When my brother, Steve, married in 1996, he and Kathy gave to each attendee a miniature wooden birdhouse. When I visited them on my way back from my 50th high-school reunion in Southern California in July 2022, I gave the birdhouse back to them.

I spent summer 1973, right after my freshman year in college as a congressional intern, working for my Southern California congressman. Initially, I didn't know a soul in Washington, DC. During my first week on the job, I was in the House of Representatives cafeteria wearing a beige sports jacket with a lapel pin of an Ichthus fish, a symbol of the Christian faith. A young woman, Loie Jo, was also a congressional intern, from Minnesota, and asked what the pin meant to me. We dated that summer and enjoyed one another's company as we visited historical sites and went to concerts. We have kept in touch as good friends for almost 50 years. In 2022, I mailed her the Ichthus pin with a note since it had brought us together initially. I can't think of a better home for the pin.

My house is far from emptied of meaningful memorabilia, letters, books, and other things of significance. I will continue to be deliberate in gifting items to people who will appreciate them. It's a way for me to spread my legacy to people who have touched my life and to preserve history.

THE
JOURNEY AHEAD

CHAPTER 35

RELIEF

"How goes the world?"
"The world goes not well, but the kingdom comes!"

Tales of the Kingdom Trilogy
David & Karen Mains

I cling onto the only life I know in hopes of extending my days and being a positive and productive influence in my world. As I think about the end of my days, missing so many things about this incredible life fills me with sadness. I still have dreams and hopes that I am not willing to shutter yet.

I find myself caught between two worlds. On the one hand, I want to be a force for good in this world and use the gifts I have been given. On the other hand, I understand that each of us will face a day of transformation from a 3D existence to a new and mysterious realm about which we know little. Such a pattern is built into the core of our humanity and is confirmed by history. That doesn't stop me from wanting to make a difference, to maintain my life for as long as I can, something also built into our humanity.

If I am honest, though, part of me will not miss this world with its pain and brokenness. When I breathe my last breath, there certainly will be a sense of relief, though clouded with the pain that likely will be present in my body. For all the essential goodness of life, we live in a shattered world filled with unspeakable suffering, violence, war, hatred, racism, poverty, and corruption, in which the unrestrained quest for money, sex, and power drives people to trample on others. This brokenness at a systemic level is also present at a personal level. For all of us, life is filled with stress and pressure. We have financial worries, relationship hassles, challenging politics at work, and health challenges. We worry about our families.

I will not miss the global and personal brokenness of this life even as I cling to it and try to positively influence the part of the world that I can influence. Death, however, will bring a sense of relief. Accordingly, we often hope those who pass away will experience peace.

In the musical "Fiddler on the Roof," Tevye sings about how time presses onward so quickly with a mixture joy and sadness: "One season following another, laden with happiness and tears."

I will not miss the tears, and there will be a sense of relief.

CHAPTER 36

JOY ON THE JOURNEY

Grant us wisdom, grant us courage,
for the facing of this hour, for the facing of this hour.
God of Grace and God of Glory hymn

Somewhere along the way, I settled on "joy on the journey" as an aspirational valediction in closing emails to friends. That doesn't mean I have arrived. Far from it. My journey is still filled with uncertainty, fears, and sadness. More than anything, however, I want to live well in the here and now and with joy on the journey in the days I do have.

We are created for an eternity we cannot comprehend with our time-bound brains. Life is too short for harboring pettiness and anger. I long to put these behind me and find joy in this final season of my life.

I want to live long and well. I am realistic enough to know that prostate cancer will likely be the final cause of my body shutting down and propelling me onto the next grand adventure. But I heed the words of Irish poet and playwright Oscar Wilde, whose life spanned just 46 years. He wrote, "To live is the rarest thing in the world. Most people just exist." I want to live well.

There are so many more people to love and care for. I will feel badly about leaving loved ones in the lurch. I am sad about the slowly developing death of my dreams and hopes. There are things I still want to write, books to read, places to visit, laughter to share with those I encounter, tears to shed with family and friends, support I want to provide for loved ones, and life to experience with my companions on this journey.

I want to live fully and faithfully in the days I am given, and to find joy in the moments of life. I want to experience spring even in the winter of my life. All we are given is the present moment before it fades into history. The future is unknown.

In some strange way that I don't really understand, I have been surprised that many friends have either written or told me that I have been inspirational to them as I navigate these uncharted waters. I am just trying to do the best I can in the present unfortunate circumstances. I feel like I am just barely hanging on at times and just doing what I need to do to keep moving forward. I am glad, however, that some people find my life to be inspirational. My hope is that they may somehow learn from me and be helped on their own journeys to live well.

To a classmate from high school, I wrote that I am "looking for joy in the moments of life on this uncertain journey." My friend responded, "Your attitude and perspective are inspirational, Mike."[74] I replied, "I certainly don't feel very inspirational." I often live in my head and try to do the right thing, although this emotional journey frequently has me sobbing with sadness.

A longtime friend from college emailed me, "Thank you for inspiring the rest of us with your strength and faith. What a journey."[75] I am grateful for my friend's words but feel neither strong nor faithful much of the time. Instead, I often worry that I won't finish the work I feel called to. I break down in tears. That doesn't feel inspirational to me. As much as is possible, however, I want my life and twilight years to be a source of encouragement to others. So, I press onward.

Another longtime friend texted me the following:

So good to talk to you today, Mike! I meant what I said about how inspiring it is that you are choosing creativity and purpose in the midst of a sucky situation. I imagine that may be hard to see from the inside, but it shines bright as day from without.[76]

My friend is right that it's hard for me to see this from the inside. I only can hope that I somehow bring inspiration to those I encounter and help people learn to live with joy on the journey.

Finding joy on the final leg of my journey is not easy. It's not for the faint of heart. Life is changing for me. I am in such a different place than I was when I turned 65, just before I was diagnosed with cancer.

In this season of life, I have experienced a loss of what I can do physically. I am not as strong or agile as I once was, and I need to be careful not to do things that might not be good for me. I recently had chimney work done on my roof. Normally, I would climb the ladder and be on the roof inspecting what work was being done. While I probably could have done it, the consequences of not being as stable on my feet and not having good balance was too big, so I didn't climb the ladder.

As my body's cells turn on themselves and replicate faster than they should, I feel discomfort I have not felt before that will, at some point, turn into pain. My treatments have impacted my energy and mobility. I cannot be as independent as I once was and need others to help me. I'm grateful for my wife, Catherine, for her ongoing support—preparing meals and taking care of household details (many of which I previously attended to) so I can focus on my health protocols, treatments, and appointments. My son has also generously helped and filled in the gaps.

I am experiencing the loss of health that I have been grateful to enjoy all my life. I now spend more time at medical appointments than I have ever done before. I work to find joy in relationships with the doctors, nurses, medical assistants, and phlebotomists, as well as my acupuncturist, naturopath, counselor, and others who serve and help me on this journey.

Even in this season of loss, I will not give up. I will work for my health as long as I can, recognizing that this is a terminal disease. I will press onward to accomplish goals and bring to fulfillment my dreams. One friend encouragingly wrote that I was doing that: "What I like most is you're living life. Building wonderful memories. Achieving book goals. You're really living!"[77]

In a strange way, facing death has broadened my capacity to experience joy. For much of my life, I have taken for granted that another day would come and that I would be healthy on that day. I have moved quickly through life and perhaps not paused to reflect on and seek joy in the moments. Out of necessity and deliberateness, I am working to find joy in all the moments of life, big and small. Not for nothing exists the cliché, "Stop and smell the roses."

CHAPTER 37

AN UNCERTAIN JOURNEY

God meets us with His presence in the high summer of life,
in the deep winter of despair, and everywhere in between.[78]

Mike Purdy

My journey ahead is quite uncertain. I don't know when God will call me home. I don't know what pain I will experience, when, or for how long. I don't know when my productive and creative days will evaporate with pain. I don't know if I will finish important things I feel called to complete.

All I know is that I live in the here and now and that each day is a new day that I am blessed with life and breath. I want to make a positive difference with the life which I have been gifted. I want to know God and love the people he's placed in my life. I want to encourage others. My life has significance eternally but it's also just a small drop in the grand arc of human history. Individual people do, however, make a difference for good or ill, and I want the measure of my days to have been positive in helping others live well.

Not only do I want to live well today, and die well when that time comes, but I also want to live without fear, even in the light of my narrowing days. I want to begin now to prepare for the next part of my journey to a new, eternal, and now mysterious existence. While I may speculate about what comes next after I breathe my last breath here, I don't know with any certainty. None of us does.

I think there is enough evidence, though, in the created order of nature and from God's character to know that what comes next will be good. As author Henri Nouwen wrote, "Not only does life lead to death, but death leads to new life."[79]

I am working to accept the seeming unfairness of being stricken with cancer at a relatively early age and while I am otherwise in excellent health. Ultimately, my identity is as one who belongs to God. He has created me and this body I am temporarily inhabiting, and he will bring me safely home to himself at the right time. Just as I didn't get to choose the date of my birth, neither will I get to choose the date of my death.

The duration of our journey is uncertain and fleeting. You may have a serious illness, or maybe a disease is developing within your body that you don't know about. Regardless of how long we live, we will all die. It's the journey of the now, with all its messiness and uncertainty, that matters. One friend wisely wrote, "Life unfolds in the moments we're in and it is enough to focus on each day as it comes."[80]

Our challenge is to live well in the moments we are given before history dissolves them from our consciousness. Perhaps living well in the moment means stepping back from the immediacy of our stress and pressure and remembering what is ultimately important: to treat others with kindness and contribute to a better world with the gifts we've been given.

An Australian Aboriginal proverb notes, "We are all visitors to this time, this place. We are just passing through. Our purpose here is to observe, to learn, to grow, to love … and then we return home."[81]

Perhaps I always should have lived as though my days on this planet were limited. Maybe I should have known better. However, something about being constrained by time deluded me into thinking there always will be another day, just like all my other previous days. It's like I had amnesia and forgot this most elemental truth of the universe. Only the shock of being diagnosed with cancer, the treatments, and the corresponding discomforts and pains that have accompanied the deterioration of my body have made me realize that I have moved into a phase of my existence defined by narrowing days.

The experience is surreal. Slowly, I am grasping the fact that the prostate cancer exploding in my body likely will be the cause of extinguishing my breath one day—this coming after a blessed lifetime of excellent health. The shock of dashed expectations has been difficult to process.

I always have known that one day my Creator would call me home. I just never expected that it would be so soon and that my health would decline so precipitously. In this season of life, I am all too aware now that the number of my future days is decreasing rapidly. Certainly, before I was diagnosed with cancer, I never knew the number of my days. I don't know that number now. I try to remind myself that what matters most is not the number of my days but the quality of my moments and my impact on others.

Since I was diagnosed with cancer in May 2019, I have ridden an endless and terrifying roller coaster. From blood tests, infusions and injections, I have had more needles poked into me than I can count. From supplements to prescription medications, I have taken a boatload of pills every day. I have had targeted radiation and chemotherapy, learned of blood clots in my leg, worn a catheter for three months, and had cataract surgery, a tooth implant, and multiple dental crowns. While some of these relate more to age than cancer, the emotional impact has been the same.

Each medical appointment has felt like my world is falling apart. Each one brings me closer to the day when treatments stop working and this body turns back to dust. Somehow, I live for another day, though I realize this can't go on like this forever. An end will come, even though I am not ready. I falsely expect and hope there will be improvement, but the nature of metastatic prostate cancer is that the aberrational cells eventually will win and take over.

While I face this ultimate uncertainty, I nevertheless press on with whatever faith I can muster, planning, hoping, dreaming, loving, and trying to live each day fully and faithfully as though I will be here for a thousand years. I am grateful I made it to my 50th high-school reunion, to connect there with classmates, and to visit family and dear friends on the drive back. Finishing this book also was a high priority for me as I hope that others may benefit from it and think more seriously about their own lives.

In saner moments when I am not overwhelmed by my medical condition, I acknowledge that faith stands in the gap between the uncertainty of my life and the certainty of knowing the character of God and that he is good. I am not afraid to die, except that I am not looking forward to the pain that will likely accompany my transition to a new world. Knowing that Jesus remains the Lord of my journey does not change my overwhelming sadness and sense of unfairness.

It's been hard to live with the constant uncertainty of my condition and how long I will live. Yet uncertainty seems to be my new normal. I don't know when my productive creativity will end. I work at accepting this uncertainty as part of the process and try to embrace each moment.

My journey is not yet over. I am in a race against time as the rogue cells continue to grow and expand in my body. Here are questions I ponder:

- How do I live well in whatever days or years God still gives to me?

- How do I live with uncertainty?

- How do I discern God's calling to me and know his heart in this final season of life?

- How do I embrace and savor each moment?

- How do I listen carefully to the deepest hopes and fears of those the Lord brings across my path?

- How do I find peace that goes beyond my craving for certainty?

- How do I gracefully go through this day in the midst of this uncertain storm?

- How do I maintain perspective and spiritual discipline when some days I feel like I am just surviving and dealing with pain and discomfort?

CHAPTER 38

ONWARD IN FAITH

Strength for today and bright hope for tomorrow.

Great is Thy Faithfulness hymn

In a strange irony, it is only when we are comfortable with our own mortality—when we realize we are time limited with an expiration date—we are then free to live fully without fear in the face of death. Our pilgrimage overflows with uncertainty, and we experience setbacks when we expect life to be free of difficulty.

While I still bemoan the unfairness of my failing health since I am not ready to leave this life, I recognize and acknowledge intellectually and theologically that when God calls me home, it will be the right time. Ultimately, we all pass from this life, and we will do so at different times and from different causes. He will give me the days to accomplish that to which he has called me. Of course, I imagine I always will bargain for just a little more time.

In light of uncertainty, I try to hold my days and my dreams lightly, recognizing each new morning of life is an unexpected gift. This experience is teaching me to live in the moment and to not delay taking actions or saying things to people I love.

Remember to say you love those in your life. We never know when it will be our last time with someone, and we don't want to have any regrets. Who we are and how we love others is our legacy to the next generation and to those who follow them.

We cannot change the length of our lives, but we can change its width, its depth, and the positive impact we have in this world. The life that fills our years, and not the length of our lives, is what counts. We can and do impact those who cross our path. May our words and actions be a reflection of God's love.

To family and dear friends who have been my companions on this grand adventure of life, I look forward to continuing our relationship in the world to come. As Ulysses S. Grant wrote in his last letter to his wife, Julia, "I bid you a final farewell until we meet in another, and I trust better, world."[82] I will look for you, my loved ones, and meet you on the other side, in another dimension, when your days are over here.

Until that day comes, my prayer is that we live our lives fully, faithfully, and gracefully, grounded in the firm knowledge that our Creator God is madly in love with us—his unique and wonderful creation—and that he will never fail or forsake us.

May God grant us the wisdom and grace to live well, love deeply, and laugh heartily, even as we experience the unknowns that confront all of us. Wishing you joy on your journey.

RESOURCES

ORGANIZATIONS

American Cancer Society

https://www.cancer.org/

Cancer Research Institute

https://www.cancerresearch.org/

National Cancer Institute

https://www.cancer.gov/

Prostate Cancer Foundation

https://www.pcf.org/

Prostate Cancer Research Institute

https://pcri.org/

National Alliance of State Prostate Cancer Coalitions

Publishes quarterly *Prostatepedia Magazine* and weekly *Prostatepedia Digests.*

https://naspcc.org/index.php/prostatepedia-magazine

URO Today

https://www.urotoday.com/

ZERO: The End of Prostate Cancer

https://zerocancer.org/

STANDARDS

National Comprehensive Cancer Network (NCCN)

- Prostate Cancer: Early Stage. https://www.nccn.org/patientresources/patient-resources/guidelines-for-patients/guidelines-for-patients-details?patientGuidelineId=49

- Prostate Cancer: Advanced Stage. https://www.nccn.org/patientresources/patient-resources/guidelines-for-patients/guidelines-for-patients-details?patientGuidelineId=50

FACEBOOK SUPPORT GROUPS

Metastatic Prostate Cancer – Prostate Cancer Foundation

https://www.facebook.com/groups/PCF.MetastaticProstateCancer

PSA Rising

https://www.facebook.com/groups/psarising

Prostate Cancer Stage 4 Defy Odds

https://www.facebook.com/groups/872135286218640

Stage 4 Prostate Cancer

https://www.facebook.com/groups/589870111167933

VIDEO

Mike Purdy sharing about cancer journey during worship service at Bethany Presbyterian Church (Seattle, Washington) on April 19, 2020, via Zoom. Go to minute 33:25 where Pastor Doug Kelly introduces me. https://subsplash.com/bethanypc/media/mi/+t9f3ydy?autoplay=true.

ACKNOWLEDGMENTS

There are many people who have walked with me on this journey and helped shape this book.

My friend, Jeff Van Duzer, originally suggested I write the book and begin to keep notes of my experiences and categorize them around large themes. He checked in with me regularly and encouraged me to keep writing. I'm appreciative for his friendship and support over many decades.

Two wonderful editors have spent countless hours to make this a significantly better book. Without their skilled editing, this book would be very cumbersome to read. My friend, Clay Eals, who has graciously edited other publications of mine, brought his decades as an editor and writer to bear on this book. I'm thankful for Clay's skills at making my writing more readable, consistent, and less redundant. You as the reader should thank him as well. Adam Lumbley lent his professional editorial skills to the book. He provided the first pass at editing the book and corrected a multitude of errors.

Painful as it sometimes is for a writer to have their work edited, Clay and Adam proved the value of a good editor who approaches a manuscript objectively. They have made me sound literate with their skilled edits, word choices, sentence structure, grammatical and punctuation fixes, and so much more. I'm indebted to both for their kind and professional assistance.

My amazingly talented son, David, designed the book's cover using both his creative and technical skills, working with a photograph (used with permission) to create a pleasing and welcoming cover. I am grateful to him for working in partnership with me on yet another book cover.

My counselor, Alyssa, provided me with perspective and wisdom that shaped my thinking as I navigated this uncertain journey. I'm grateful for her gracious spirit on this journey.

Friends have allowed me to process with them many of the concepts in this book. They helped me refine my thinking, and I'm indebted to them for their love, support, and encouragement.

My wife, Catherine, provided time for me to get away frequently on retreats to write this book. Without such focused time, I would still be working on Chapter 1.

NOTES

1. *Telling Secrets*, by Frederick Buechner (San Francisco: HarperCollins Publishers, 1991), p. 30.

2. Marcy Hunter, Aug. 5, 2021.

3. Mike Purdy's journal, July 28, 2021.

4. *Our Greatest Gift: A Meditation on Dying and Caring*, by Henri J. M. Nouwen (New York: HarperCollins Publishers, 1994), p. xvi.

5. Text from Anne Marie Baer, Oct. 29, 2021.

6. Mike Purdy, from article submitted to *Christianity Today* for "The Bible: Faith and Work" edition, December 7, 2014.

7. *Mere Christianity*, by C.S. Lewis (New York: The Macmillan Company, 1972), p. 123.

8. Mike Purdy's journal, Oct. 4, 2019.

9. Some test standards peg a normal PSA at less than 4.0.

10. *101 Presidential Insults: What They Really Thought About Each Other – and What It Means to Us*, by Mike Purdy.

11. https://www.uspreventiveservicestaskforce.org/uspstf/recommendation/prostate-cancer-screening.

12. "Fallout" from New Study: Men with Early Balding May Be at Higher Risk of Aggressive Prostate Cancer, by Janet Farrar Worthington, Prostate Cancer Foundation, https://www.pcf.org/c/fallout-from-new-study-men-with-early-balding-may-be-at-higher-risk-of-aggressive-prostate-cancer/.

13. *Winter of the World*, by Ken Follett (Penguin Books, 2014).

14. Plant-Based Diets and Prostate Cancer, by Prostate Cancer Foundation, https://zerocancer.org/blog/progress-in-prostate-cancer-research-plant-based-diets-and-prostate-cancer/.

15. https://pubmed.ncbi.nlm.nih.gov/29140493/.

16.   https://www.fda.gov/consumers/consumer-updates/hyperbaric-oxy-gen-therapy-get-facts

17.   *2022 Prostate Cancer Advanced Stage*, NCCN Guidelines for Patients, https://www.nccn.org/patients/guidelines/content/PDF/prostate-ad-vanced-patient.pdf.

18.   Email from Cindy Tyran on July 21, 2021.

19.   Text from Marcy Hunter on July 1, 2022.

20.   Mike Purdy's journal, June 8, 2019.

21.   Testosterone blocking injection. Mike Purdy's journal, June 8, 2019.

22.   Psalm 139:16.

23.   Henry F. Pringle, *The Life and Times of William Howard Taft*, Volume 1 (New York: Farrar & Rinehart, Inc., 1939), p. 107.

24.   https://anthonybergen.medium.com/blister-the-day-calvin-coolidge-lost-his-favorite-son-and-his-passion-for-the-presidency-fe7b6b638f.

25.   *The Autobiography of Calvin Coolidge*, by Calvin Coolidge (New York: Cosmopolitan Book Corporation, 1931), p. 190.

26.   https://www.census.gov/quickfacts/fact/table/US/PST045221.

27.   Anne Marie Baer text on June 23, 2022.

28.   *Now and Then: A Memoir of Vocation*, by Frederick Buechner (San Francisco: HarperCollins Publishers, 1991), p. 87.

29.   *101 Presidential Insults: What They Really Thought About Each Other and What It Means to Us* (June 7, 2019) and *Presidential Friendships: How They Changed History* (Aug. 3, 2022).

30.   From *Every Moment Holy, Volume 2: Death, Grief, and Hope,* by Douglas Kaine McKelvey, Copyright 2020 by Douglas Kaine McKelvey, Used with permission. www.EveryMomentHoly.com, pp. 73-75.

31.   https://peacefullyharsh.com/tag/fiddler-on-the-roof/.

32.   Christine Leeming on March 12, 2022.

33.   John 11:35.

34.   From planned anthology by Mike Purdy on "Maintaining Your Spiritual Vitality," 1990.

35.   Come Thou Fount on Every Blessing

36.   Come Thou Fount on Every Blessing

37.   Blessed Assurance

38.   Blessed Assurance

39. O For a Thousand Tongues to Sing

40. O For a Thousand Tongues to Sing

41. O Come O Come Emmanuel

42. O Come O Come Emmanuel

43. Guide Me O Thou Great Jehovah

44. Guide Me O Thou Great Jehovah

45. Lead on O King Eternal

46. Who is on the Lord's Side?

47. God of Grace and God of Glory

48. Love Divine All Loves Excelling

49. Be Still My Soul

50. Dave Baab on June 16, 2019.

51. Christine Leeming on March 23, 2022.

52. From talk by Mike Purdy at Bethany Presbyterian Church, Seattle, Washington, April 19, 2020.

53. Mike Purdy's journal, Dec. 6, 2019.

54. C.S. Lewis letter to Mary Willis Shelburne, June 17, 1963. *The Collected Letters of C.S. Lewis,* Volume 3.

55. Email from Cindy Tyran.

56. *The Longing for Home*, by Frederick Buechner (San Francisco: HarperCollins Publishers, 1996), p. 1.

57. *The Last Battle*, by C.S. Lewis (New York: Collier Books, 1976), p. 184.

58. *Becoming: Your Self in the Making*, by Calvin Miller (Old Tappan, New Jersey: Fleming H. Revell Company, 1987).

59. Matthew 6:26.

60. Joyful, Joyful We Adore Thee hymn.

61. Facebook Messenger text from Christine Leeming on Feb. 23, 2022.

62. Signed card by Vice President George H.W. Bush to Ruth and Chuck Lieb, June 14, 1986.

63. *Devotions upon Emergent Occasions*, a 1624 prose work by English poet John Donne.

64. James Langland, editor, *The Chicago Daily News Almanac and Year-Book for 1919*. Woodrow Wilson speech on May 18, 1918, at the Metropolitan Opera house in New York City for Red Cross fundraising event. (Chicago: The Chicago Daily News Company, 1918), p. 406. https://www.google.com/

books/edition/The_Chicago_Daily_News_Almanac_and_Yearb/f6l-dsvn-jhEC?hl=en&gbpv=1&dq=%22Friendship+is+the+only+cement%22&p-g=PA406&printsec=frontcover

65. *The Lincoln Treasury* by Caroline Thomas Harnsberger (Chicago: Wilcox & Follett Co. 1950). p. 108. From a letter to Joseph Gillespie. Springfield, Ill, July 13, 1849.

66. Benjamin Harrison Presidential Site. https://bhpsite.org/old-glory-new-vision/

67. Email from Cindy Tyran, Aug. 25, 2022.

68. John Schaufelberger, Professor of Construction Management, University of Washington.

69. *Grace in the Wilderness: The Heart and Mind of Mike Purdy (Selected Writings – Volume 1: Life and Work)*, p. 280.

70. The content from these Christmas Eve and other worship services I have led at Bethany Presbyterian Church in Seattle, Washington is included in my book, *Grace in the Wilderness: The Heart and Mind of Mike Purdy (Selected Writings – Volume 3: Theology)*. Also included in the book are sermons I have preached, and the content of adult Christian education classes I have taught.

71. Mike Purdy's journal, Dec. 13, 2019.

72. The Akron Public Library collection contains some 7,500 books, CDs, DVDs, and other items. My personal library consists of approximately 6,000 books. https://coloradoencyclopedia.org/article/akron-public-library.

73. *Thoughts and Adventures: Churchill Reflects on Spies, Cartoons, Flying, and the Future*, by Winston S. Churchill, p. 318.

74. Facebook Messenger text from Carol Marriott Grover on March 12, 2022.

75. Email from Cindy Tyran, Feb. 26, 2022.

76. Text from Kimberlee Conway Ireton on Feb. 24, 2022, after Zoom call.

77. Text from Anne Marie Baer, July 23, 2022.

78. Mike Purdy's note to a friend, March 18, 2010.

79. *Our Greatest Gift: A Meditation on Dying and* Caring, by Henri Nouwen (New York: HarperCollins Publishers, 1994), p. xv.

80. Text from Hejsa Christensen, May 22, 2020.

81. https://www.quotes.net/quote/16576.

82. June 29, 1885.